8 studies from First Peter on living with hope and courage in the midst of difficult times

by M. Scott Miles

A DIVISION OF SCRIPTURE PRESS PUBLICATIONS INC.
USA CANADA ENGLAND

Scripture quotations are from the *Holy Bible, New International Version®*. Copyright © 1973, 1978, 1984 by International Bible Society. Used by permission of Zondervan Publishing House. All rights reserved.

Recommended Dewey Decimal Classification: 301.402
Suggested Subject Heading: SMALL GROUPS

Library of Congress Catalog Card Number:
ISBN: 1-56476-104-5

1 2 3 4 5 6 7 8 9 10 Printing/Year 97 96 95 94 93

VICTOR BOOKS
A division of SP Publications, Inc.
Wheaton, Illinois 60187

CONTENTS

PURPOSE: To help believers experience the hope and courage of Jesus Christ in the midst of suffering, pain, and difficult times.

INTRODUCTION

When the Walls Are Closing In is for people who want to experience the hope and courage of Jesus Christ in the midst of their suffering, pain, and difficult times. An in-depth Leader's Guide is included at the back of the book with suggested time guidelines to help you structure your emphases. Each of the 8 sessions contains the following elements:

❑ **GroupSpeak**—quotes from group members that capsulize what the session is about.

❑ **Getting Acquainted**—activities or selected readings to help you begin thinking and sharing from your life and experiences about the subject of the session. Use only those options that seem appropriate for your group.

❑ **Gaining Insight**—questions and in-depth Bible study help you gain principles from Scripture for life-related application.

❑ **Growing By Doing**—an opportunity to practice the Truth learned in the Gaining Insight section.

❑ **Going The Second Mile**—a personal enrichment section for you to do on your own.

❑ **Growing As A Leader**—an additional section in the Leader's Guide for the development and assessment of leadership skills.

❑ **Pocket Principles**—brief guidelines inserted in the Leader's Guide to help the Group Leader learn small group leadership skills as needed.

❑ **Session Objectives**—goals listed in the Leader's Guide that describe what should happen in the group by the end of the session.

IS THIS YOUR FIRST SMALL GROUP?

'smol grüp: A limited number of individuals assembled together having some unifying relationship.

Kris'chen 'smol grüp: 4–12 persons who meet together on a regular basis, over a determined period of time, for the shared purpose of pursuing biblical truth. They seek to mature in Christ and become equipped to serve as His ministers in the world.

Picture Your First Small Group.

List some words that describe what you want your small group to look like.

What Kind Of Small Group Do You Have?

People form all kinds of groups based on gender, age, marital status, and so forth. There are advantages and disadvantages to each. Here are just a few:

- ❑ **Same Age Groups** will probably share similar needs and interests.

- ❑ **Intergenerational Groups** bring together people with different perspectives and life experiences.
- ❑ **Men's or Women's Groups** usually allow greater freedom in sharing and deal with more focused topics.
- ❑ **Singles or Married Groups** determine their relationship emphases based on the needs of a particular marital status.
- ❑ **Mixed Gender Groups (singles and/or couples)** stimulate interaction and broaden viewpoints while reflecting varied lifestyles.

However, the most important area of "alikeness" to consider when forming a group is an **agreed-on purpose.** Differences in purpose will sabotage your group and keep its members from bonding. If, for example, Mark wants to pray but not play while Jan's goal is to learn through playing, then Mark and Jan's group will probably not go anywhere. People need different groups at different times in their lives. Some groups will focus on sharing and accountability, some on work projects or service, and others on worship. *Your small group must be made up of persons who have similar goals.*

How Big Should Your Small Group Be?

The **fewest** people to include would be **4.** Accountability will be high, but absenteeism may become a problem.

The **most** to include would be **12.** But you will need to subdivide regularly into groups of 3 or 4 if you want people to feel cared for and to have time for sharing.

How Long Should You Meet?

8 Weeks gives you a start toward becoming a close community, but doesn't overburden busy schedules. Count on needing three or four weeks to develop a significant trust level. The smaller the group, the more quickly trust develops.

Weekly Meetings will establish bonding at a good pace and allow for accountability. The least you can meet and still be an effective group is once a month. If you choose the latter, work at individual contact among group members between meetings.

You will need **75 minutes** to accomplish a quality meeting. The larger the size, the more time it takes to become a healthy group. Serving refreshments will add 20–30 minutes, and singing and/or prayer time, another 20–30 minutes. Your time duration may be determined by the time of day you meet and by the amount of energy members bring to the group. Better to start small and ask for more time when it is needed because of growth.

What Will Your Group Do?

To be effective, each small group meeting should include:

1. **Sharing**—You need to share who you are and what is happening in your life. This serves as a basis for relationship building and becomes a springboard for searching out scriptural truth.

2. **Scripture**—There must always be biblical input from the Lord to teach, rebuke, correct, and train in right living. Such material serves to move your group in the direction of maturity in Christ and protects from pooled ignorance and distorted introspection.

3. **Truth in practice**—It is vital to provide opportunities for *doing* the Word of God. Experiencing this within the group insures greater likelihood that insights gained will be utilized in everyday living.

Other elements your group may wish to add to these three are: a time of **worship**, **specific prayer** for group members, **shared projects**, a time to **socialize** and enjoy **refreshments**, and **recreation.**

ONE

Seeing Hope Through the Hurt

GroupSpeak: *"While I'm not what you would call a pessimist, there are times when I don't feel very hopeful about things—specifically or generally. This is a good reminder for me."*

Tough Times and Tough People

"Tough times don't last, tough people do!" Ever hear that before? Whether you agree with the statement or not, there is a grain of truth in it. Tough people generally do outlast tough times, but not because they are *tough.* Tough people outlast tough times because they are people who have hope. People who have hope can stand confidently when the walls begin to close in on them.

A simple fact of life is that sooner or later, the walls will close in on you. Sometimes you might even feel like the roof is caving in. Life is tough stuff. No one is exempt from pain and suffering. Hopelessness is a natural response. For many, it is the only response. However, it does not have to be. It is possible to see hope through the hurt of hard times. In the Book of 1 Peter, we read about people who knew how tough life can be. Even in their hurt, they had hope. You can too!

GETTING ACQUAINTED

Crossing Words
Beginning with letters from the word *hope,* make a crossword puzzle design with words or short phrases that describe or define what hope is for Christians.

H

O

P

E

The fun is just beginning! Try writing a statement about *hope* using the words and phrases you listed in the crossword exercise.

GAINING INSIGHT

Going through tough times can sometimes make us feel insecure. However, the message of Jesus Christ is that there is hope—hope that is based on something real and eternal. When a Christian loses that sense of hope in Jesus Christ, he or she loses something foundational to being a Christian. More importantly, this person will lose hold of the very thing that can give him/her security when he/she is hurting. Peter can help us see hope through our hurts.

People Who Have Hope
Do you feel very hopeful when the walls start closing in on you? The people to whom Peter wrote were people who were experiencing pain and suffering. Yet, they had hope. Read 1 Peter 1:1-2. As you read, circle the words that describe the people to whom Peter wrote.

[1]Peter, an apostle of Jesus Christ, to God's elect, strangers in the world, scattered throughout Pontus, Galatia, Cappadocia, Asia and Bithynia, [2]who have been chosen according to

the foreknowledge of God the Father, by the sanctifying work of the Spirit, for obedience to Jesus Christ and sprinkling by His blood: Grace and peace be yours in abundance.

1 Peter 1:1-2

From the words you circled as you read, how would you describe the pain and suffering these believers have experienced?

Peter's readers had indeed experienced a great deal of suffering. However, they had good reason to be hopeful. Peter describes the reason for their hope in two ways. First, he calls them *chosen.* What do you think he means?

Think of a time when you were especially chosen by someone for something special. How did that make you feel about yourself and about your circumstances?

Peter also describes his readers as *strangers* and *scattered.* In what ways are Peter's readers strangers in the world?

Realizing that we are not attached to this physical world in which we live is an important aspect of a Christian's hope. Read the following Scriptures. Paraphrase what each one has to say about the hope believers have because we are strangers in this world.

[12]"Hear my prayer, O Lord, listen to my cry for help; be not deaf to my weeping. For I dwell with You as an alien, a stranger, as all my fathers were."

Psalm 39:12

Paraphrase:

[20]But our citizenship is in heaven. And we eagerly await a Savior from there, the Lord Jesus Christ, [21]who, by the power that enables Him to bring everything under His control, will transform our lowly bodies so that they will be like His glorious body.

Philippians 3:20-21

Paraphrase:

**8By faith Abraham, when called to go to a place he would
later receive as his inheritance, obeyed and went, even
though he did not know where he was going. 9By faith he
made his home in the promised land like a stranger in a
foreign country; he lived in tents, as did Isaac and Jacob,
who were heirs with him of the same promise. 10For he was
looking forward to the city with foundations, whose archi-
tect and builder is God.**

Hebrews 11:8-10

Paraphrase:

How should these truths of being chosen and strangers make us feel about ourselves when the walls start closing in on us?

Reasons Why Hope Is Real

According to Peter, the believer's hope is anchored firmly in the salvation we have through the work of Jesus Christ. From beginning to end, Peter gives us a tremendous picture of this salvation we enjoy in Christ. Read 1 Peter 1:3-5, 10-12.

**3Praise be to the God and Father of our Lord Jesus Christ!
In His great mercy He has given us new birth into a living
hope through the resurrection of Jesus Christ from the
dead, 4and into an inheritance that can never perish, spoil
or fade—kept in heaven for you, 5who through faith are
shielded by God's power until the coming of the salvation
that is ready to be revealed in the last time.**

**10Concerning this salvation, the prophets, who spoke of the
grace that was to come to you, searched intently and
with the greatest care, 11trying to find out the time and
circumstances to which the Spirit of Christ in them was
pointing when He predicted the sufferings of Christ and
the glories that would follow. 12It was revealed to them that
they were not serving themselves but you, when they
spoke of the things that have now been told you by those**

who have preached the gospel to you by the Holy Spirit sent from heaven. Even angels long to look into these things.

1 Peter 1:3-5, 10-12

List the main points Peter makes about our salvation in Jesus Christ.

On what is this salvation based?

Review what Peter says in verses 10-12. What the prophets said about Jesus they said just for you. Even the angels long to look into all that we have received through Jesus Christ! After reading what Peter says in these verses, circle three words from the list below to describe how it makes you feel.

happy	secure	confident
important	special	significant
warm	excited	grateful
needed	thankful	anxious
expectant	joyful	restful

How does all that Peter says about your salvation give you a sense of hope in the midst of hurtful times?

What Hope Can Do

This great salvation we have in Christ not only gives us a living hope for the future, but it serves as our anchor in life now. This living hope can transform our lives, and help us see through all our present hurts. Read 1 Peter 1:6-9.

**6In this you greatly rejoice, though now for a little while
you may have had to suffer grief in all kinds of trials.
7These have come so that your faith—of greater worth
than gold, which perishes even though refined by fire—
may be proved genuine and may result in praise, glory
and honor when Jesus Christ is revealed. 8Though you
have not seen Him, you love Him; and even though you**

do not see Him now, you believe in Him and are filled with an inexpressible and glorious joy, [9]for you are receiving the goal of your faith, the salvation of your souls.

1 Peter 1:6-9

According to Peter, how should your hope in Christ impact your perspective of what you experience in your life now?

What is God's purpose in allowing pain and hurt to enter your life?

How does God's purpose relate to the goal of our faith that Peter talks about in verse 9?

What can you learn from this passage to help you cope with the hurt you may be experiencing in your life now?

GROWING BY DOING

Discovering Your Hope

As you reflect upon how your hope in Christ applies to what you are experiencing in your life now, try this creative writing exercise. Complete the following sentence with specific information about several difficult situations you now face, and how Peter's words of hope apply to each circumstance.

"Hope is ______________________________,

when ______________________________."

Optional—Having a Hopeful Outlook

Every situation you face, particularly the difficult ones, can seem hopeless or hopeful, depending on your perspective. Consider your perspective of the difficult situations in your life by completing the following exercise.

❑ A difficult situation I now face is:

❑ This could feel like a hopeless situation because (list up to 3 reasons):

❑ Three things from this study I need to remember that will help me be hopeful in the midst of this situation are:

GOING THE SECOND MILE

Spend a few minutes this week planning how you can share a word of hope with someone else. Who do you know that needs to hear a word of living hope in the midst of their circumstances? In the space below, outline a brief letter of hope that you will write to encourage this person based on this Bible study. Then write and hand deliver your "word of hope" to him/her.

Person needing a word of hope:

Encouragements from this study I will share with him/her:

TWO

Staying Clean When Things Get Dirty

GroupSpeak: *"I guess I always just thought staying clean (or holy) was a responsibility, kind of a Christian duty. To think of it as a response to what Jesus did for me, well, that's kind of liberating."*

Living Above It All

Our world is a dirty place to live. Indeed, during tough times, it can be difficult to live above the filth and corruption we see around us. In fact, suffering can sometimes tempt us to make our own justice by participating in the worldly ways we see around us. But, Peter says, there is a better way. The Christian participates in a glorious hope in Jesus Christ. That hope should motivate us to live a life worthy of this eternal hope. In other words, we should stay clean when things get dirty.

So, how do we stay clean when things around us are so dirty? In a very practical statement, Peter gives us four basic principles to help us.

GETTING ACQUAINTED

Which Is Worse?

The world today is definitely in a mess! There seems to be no end of wrong for people to do. Just look at the list below.

As you do, try to rank these items from one to twenty, starting with the absolute worst and ending with the, well, not quite as bad as the others.

___ spouse abuse	___ blackmail
___ drinking	___ prostitution
___ pornography	___ drugs
___ embezzlement	___ homosexuality
___ profanity	___ fraud
___ child abuse	___ smoking
___ murder	___ rape
___ armed robbery	___ gang wars
___ incest	___ dirty jokes
___ lying	___ abortion

GAINING INSIGHT

For the Christian, hope in the midst of hurt is a very real thing. As Christians we enjoy a wonderful assurance of salvation because of our faith in Jesus Christ and because of God's mercy. But there is another side to that coin. Sharing in such a glorious hope does not mean we can presume on God's great grace. Rather, we should respond by staying clean when things get dirty. Let's look at the challenge Peter gives us.

Developing Mental Discipline

The first challenge Peter gives us has to do with the way we think. *How* we think is just as important as *what* we think. Read 1 Peter 1:13.

[13]Therefore, prepare your minds for action; be self-controlled; set your hope fully on the grace to be given you when Jesus Christ is revealed.

1 Peter 1:13

Peter's phrase, "prepare your minds for action," refers to a man tying up his robe with a belt in preparation to run, work, or do something requiring physical movement. The modern equivalent is rolling up your sleeves to get to work. Peter is obviously telling us that it takes work to discipline our minds. Do you agree or disagree? Why?

How does having a disciplined mind affect our ability to stay clean in a dirty world?

Think about it. What impacts the way you think? What are those things around you that can have an unhealthy influence on your mind? Look over the list below. Check the three things that have the most influence on the way you think.

___ television	___ music	___ best friend
___ billboard ads	___ spouse	___ magazines
___ family/relatives	___ books	___ church
___ next-door neighbor	___ videos	___ friends
___ movies	___ radio	___ newspaper
___ work environment		

Now, evaluate the impact these three things have on the way you think. Is it positive, negative, or neutral? Or perhaps it is both positive and negative. List your three things on the lines below. Circle the number to indicate the kind of impact these items have on your thinking.

____

-4 -3 -2 -1 0 +1 +2 +3 +4

____

-4 -3 -2 -1 0 +1 +2 +3 +4

____

-4 -3 -2 -1 0 +1 +2 +3 +4

What is the relationship between a disciplined mind and setting your hope on the grace you will receive when Jesus returns?

List a few ways you can overcome the negative influences that challenge your mental discipline.

Practicing Obedience

For those who want to stay clean in a dirty world, obedience is clearly a central issue. Read 1 Peter 1:14-16 and 4:1-3.

[14]As obedient children, do not conform to the evil desires you had when you lived in ignorance. [15]But just as He who called you is holy, so be holy in all you do; [16]for it is written: "Be holy, because I am holy."

1 Peter 1:14-16

[1]Therefore, since Christ suffered in His body, arm yourselves also with the same attitude, because he who has suffered in his body is done with sin. [2]As a result, he does not live the rest of his earthly life for evil human desires, but rather for the will of God. [3]For you have spent enough time in the past doing what pagans choose to do—living in debauchery, lust, drunkenness, orgies, carousing and detestable idolatry.

1 Peter 4:1-3

Analyze what it means to be holy. List what we should do and what we should not do to live obediently in holiness, according to Peter.

DO	DO NOT DO

How should the nature of God influence the way we live?

What was Christ's attitude toward suffering?

What does it mean to arm yourself with Christ's attitude?

Are there certain areas of your life where your obedience to God is most likely to be challenged? Note *what* and *how* in the space below. Then state how you can respond appropriately to these challenges, based on these words from Peter.

Recognize the Judgment of God

Generally, we think of God's judgment as a negative thing. But, according to Peter, God's judgment can be a very positive force in the life of a Christian—especially when things get dirty. Read 1 Peter 1:17 and 4:4-6.

[17]Since you call on a Father who judges each man's work impartially, live your lives as strangers here in reverent fear.

1 Peter 1:17

[4]They think it strange that you do not plunge with them into the same flood of dissipation, and they heap abuse on you. [5]But they will have to give account to Him who is ready to judge the living and the dead. [6]For this is the reason the gospel was preached even to those who are now dead, so that they might be judged according to men in regard to the body, but live according to God in regard to the spirit.

1 Peter 4:4-6

In relation to His own children, what kind of judge is God? What conclusions can you draw from Peter's description of God as a *"Father* who judges"?

Once again Peter refers to Christians as strangers in the world. How does the idea of being strangers in the world relate to the idea of God judging our lives?

Live As One Redeemed

Peter's thoughts once again focus on the great salvation we have in Jesus Christ. This time, however, he has a different emphasis. Previously he talked about the assurance and hope of our salvation. Here he deals with the price of our salvation. We need, therefore, to take special note of what he tells us. Read 1 Peter 1:18-21.

**18For you know that it was not with perishable things such
as silver or gold that you were redeemed from the empty
way of life handed down to you from your forefathers, 19but
with the precious blood of Christ, a lamb without blemish
or defect. 20He was chosen before the creation of the
world, but was revealed in these last times for your sake.
21Through Him you believe in God, who raised Him from
the dead and glorified Him, and so your faith and hope
are in God.**

1 Peter 1:18-21

Once again, list the points Peter makes about our salvation in Jesus Christ.

Now focus your attention specifically on Jesus. What role did He play, and what did it cost Him?

The price God paid to redeem us from sin is foundational for challenging us to stay clean in a dirty world. Reflect on just what this means to you. How should the cost of your redemption affect the way you live?

GROWING BY DOING

Raising the Stakes

In response to the challenges Peter gives for staying clean when things get dirty, what commitments can you make? Look over the four principles below. Write down one commitment you can make to build each one into your daily spiritual experience.

In order to stay clean in a dirty world, I commit myself to:

Live with mental preparedness and discipline by . . .

Live as an obedient child of God who does not conform to unhealthy desires by . . .

Live under the judgment of God by . . .

Live as one who has been redeemed at a great cost by . . .

GOING THE SECOND MILE

Review and reflect on the commitment(s) you made in the Growing By Doing section. Even the best made plans and intentions can be sidetracked. Read the following Scripture passages. Summarize what each one teaches about God's commitment to you. Then spend a few minutes contemplating how God's commitment to you can help you keep your commitments to Him.

**[8]He will keep you strong to the end, so that you will be
blameless on the day of our Lord Jesus Christ. [9]God, who
has called you into fellowship with His Son Jesus Christ our
Lord, is faithful.**

1 Corinthians 1:8-9

**[12]That is why I am suffering as I am. Yet I am not ashamed,
because I know whom I have believed, and am convinced that He is able to guard what I have entrusted to
Him for that day.**

2 Timothy 1:12

**[24]To Him who is able to keep you from falling and to
present you before His glorious presence without fault and
with great joy—[25]to the only God our Savior be glory, maj-
esty, power and authority, through Jesus Christ our Lord,
before all ages, now and forevermore! Amen.**

Jude 24-25

THREE

Becoming the Person God Is Making You

GroupSpeak: *"You know, I've always been told that when things get rough you should ask what God wants to teach you, rather than why things happen. But, actually, it makes more sense to ask what kind of person God wants me to become. That really does bring things into sharper focus."*

Your Kind of People

What kind of people do you enjoy being around? Most of us have some sort of standard by which we evaluate those we choose to include in our circle of friends. Usually it is unspoken, and many times undefinable. We may not even realize we are measuring people the way we do. Even so, we all have that part of us that wants to be with people who are *our kind of people.*

God has His standards too. He wants us to be *His kind of people.* But unlike our standard, God's standard has to do with the kind of person He desires to see us become. During those times of pain and suffering, He will work in our lives to mold us into His kind of people. For, in the tough times, we are generally more pliable than in the good times. We are more open to learning from God. This is primarily because, in the painful times, our hearts are searching hard to make sense out of what we are experiencing.

When the walls are closing in on you, what kind of person does God want you to become?

GETTING ACQUAINTED

The Ideal You

What would it be like to be able to change yourself into the kind of person you have always dreamed of being? Think about it—the ultimate makeover! Don't limit yourself to what is possible, just have some fun with the idea. Fill in the space below with the information requested. Go ahead, make your day!

If I could make myself over to be whoever and whatever I wanted, I would . . .

- ❑ have an IQ of:
- ❑ look like:
- ❑ have an annual income of:
- ❑ establish a career as:
- ❑ spend my leisure time:
- ❑ live in:
- ❑ be married to:
- ❑ take my dream vacation in:
- ❑ drive a:
- ❑ have as my best friends:
- ❑ be involved in the community by:
- ❑ attend church at:

Now think for a moment. How does this ideal stack up to the kind of person you believe God wants to make you into right now?

GAINING INSIGHT

When times get tough, and the walls are closing in, who should you try to be? Better yet, what kind of person is God trying to make you into? God is not interested in the ultimate makeover of your life. He is, however, concerned that while you are walking through the painful times you are aware of what He wants to do inside you. Peter was aware of five personal character traits that he believed were primary for people in pain. Let's see how we stack up.

Loving People

Peter challenges his readers to work harder than they ever have before at being people who love each other. Read 1 Peter 1:22–2:1.

22Now that you have purified yourselves by obeying the
truth so that you have sincere love for your brothers, love
one another deeply, from the heart. 23For you have been
born again, not of perishable seed, but of imperishable,
through the living and enduring word of God. 24For, "All
men are like grass, and all their glory is like the flowers of
the field; the grass withers and the flowers fall, 25but the
word of the Lord stands forever." And this is the word that
was preached to you.

1Therefore, rid yourselves of all malice and all deceit, hypocrisy, envy, and slander of every kind.

1 Peter 1:22–2:1

Peter uses two different words for *love* in verse 22. When speaking of sincere love, he uses the word *phile,* which refers to human affection and fondness, or attachment by preference. It is the kind of pleasure we have with another person because we like their personality, or because of things we have in common. But when speaking of loving deeply, Peter changes to the word *agape,* the kind of love that can only come from God. It is a kind of love that continually seeks after the best welfare of others, irrespective of who or what they are. What then is Peter saying? How are we to love each other?

According to Peter, what is the basis for this kind of love between Christians?

In verse 1 of chapter 2, Peter lists a number of things that create barriers to the kind of love believers are to have for each other. In the lines below, list each one. Then note how each one creates a barrier to loving other Christians with God's kind of love.

Based on what Peter has said, try this exercise. Complete the following sentence with two or three specific statements, reflecting both positive actions and negative barriers to being loving people.

To love each other sincerely and deeply from the heart means . . .

TO ________________ RATHER THAN ______________

TO ________________ RATHER THAN ______________

TO ________________ RATHER THAN ______________

Growing Babies

Peter uses an interesting image to describe the kind of people into whom God is making us. Usually, we tell people to grow up and act like adults. But, in the next verse, Peter tells Christians to be like babies. Read 1 Peter 2:2-3.

[2]Like newborn babies, crave pure spiritual milk, so that by it you may grow up in your salvation, [3]now that you have tasted that the Lord is good.

1 Peter 2:2-3

According to Peter, in what way are Christians like newborn babies?

What does the word "crave" mean? What is "pure spiritual milk"? Why should we want to have spiritual nourishment so badly?

Living Stones

Peter presents his next character trait as if it were a fine jewel. There are many facets, but each facet serves to define a single image. Read 1 Peter 2:4-8.

4As you come to Him, the living Stone—rejected by men
but chosen by God and precious to Him— 5you also, like
living stones, are being built into a spiritual house to be a
holy priesthood, offering spiritual sacrifices acceptable to
God through Jesus Christ. 6For in Scripture it says: "See, I
lay a stone in Zion, a chosen and precious cornerstone,
and the one who trusts in Him will never be put to shame."
7Now to you who believe, this stone is precious. But to
those who do not believe, "The stone the builders rejected
has become the capstone," 8and, "A stone that causes
men to stumble and a rock that makes them fall."

1 Peter 2:4-8

Peter says a great deal about Jesus in these verses. He even quotes from three passages in the Old Testament: Isaiah 28:16, Psalm 118:22, and Isaiah 8:14. Try to briefly paraphrase what Peter is telling us about Jesus in these verses.

We are like Jesus. He is the living Stone. We too are living stones. As living stones, God wants to do something special with us. Look at the three descriptive phrases Peter uses. What do you think of when you read each one? As you reflect on what each one means, jot down any images or ideas that come to your mind.

- ❑ Built into a spiritual house
- ❑ To be a holy priesthood
- ❑ Offering spiritual sacrifices

How well do you exhibit these various facets of being a living stone? Evaluate yourself. Place an X at the point where you see yourself between each pair of opposites.

spiritual house

solid ______________________________ crumbling

holy priesthood

serving ______________________________ avoiding

spiritual sacrifices

hot ______________________________ cold

Testifying Witnesses

While God's work in the life of a Christian involves many things, His purpose for us is always singular. Read 1 Peter 2:9-10.

9But you are a chosen people, a royal priesthood, a holy nation, a people belonging to God, that you may declare the praises of Him who called you out of darkness into His wonderful light. 10Once you were not a people, but now you are the people of God; once you had not received mercy, but now you have received mercy.

1 Peter 2:9-10

Peter uses a number of phrases to describe who we are as Christians—chosen people, royal priesthood, holy nation, people belonging to God, the people of God. Wow! What a glorious new life God has given us! Think about it. What do these phrases tell us about the relationship we have with Jesus Christ, and with each other?

Peter states that God has brought us out of darkness into His wonderful light. As you reflect on what God has done in your life, is there a personal darkness out of which God has brought you? Note it below and share it with your small group.

Why has God done all of this for us?

As Christians, perhaps we do not always do well in declaring the praises of God to those around us. But according to Peter, this is God's primary intention in saving us. List one practical idea for how you can better declare the praises of God...

in daily life at home ______________________________

in relationships at work ___________________________

in leisure times with friends _______________________

Distinctive Saints

Peter once again picks up a familiar theme, but with a new twist. Read 1 Peter 2:11-12.

[11]Dear friends, I urge you, as aliens and strangers in the world, to abstain from sinful desires, which war against your soul. [12]Live such good lives among the pagans that, though they accuse you of doing wrong, they may see your good deeds and glorify God on the day He visits us.

1 Peter 2:11-12

This world is not our home. We do not belong here and are easy targets for those looking for someone to accuse. Therefore, we need to be careful how we live. Describe the kind of life Peter says Christians are to live in the world.

What reason(s) does Peter give for Christians to be such distinctive people?

Being distinctive is easy when the issues are black and white. But, what about the gray areas we encounter. So often, this is where Christians can make a positive difference in their environment. Think about one gray area you now face. Work through the exercise below to help you sharpen your distinctiveness.

❑ One gray area I now face is:

❑ Reasons this is not bad or not wrong:

❑ Reasons why this can be considered bad or wrong:

❑ The appropriate response that would help me be distinctively Christian is:

GROWING BY DOING

What Kind of Person Am I Becoming?
When you are in the midst of painful times, how well do you demonstrate these five character qualities? Take this simple test to determine how you can improve your growth response to God during your difficult times.

When I am in the midst of painful times, I am a . . .	Always (4)	Sometimes (3)	Seldom (2)	Never (1)
loving person	___	___	___	___
growing baby	___	___	___	___
living stone	___	___	___	___
testifying witness	___	___	___	___
distinctive saint	___	___	___	___

Now add your total score: ______

Based on your score, check the statement below that applies to your overall performance:

a. ___ Doing fine
b. ___ Doing okay, but could adjust a few things
c. ___ Need to make a number of changes
d. ___ Really have to do some things differently
e. ___ Not doing well at all! Need to evaluate everything

The one quality I probably need the most help with is:

Conclude by making some GROWTH RESPONSE PLANS. Complete the following sentence.

Three things I can do to improve my growth response to God in this area are:

GOING THE SECOND MILE

Spend some time this week contemplating the three action plans you made at the end of the session. Are there any roadblocks or barriers preventing you from putting your plan into action? What are they? Write them below and determine how to deal with each one.

	ROADBLOCK	REMOVING THE BLOCK
GROWTH RESPONSE #1		
GROWTH RESPONSE #2		
GROWTH RESPONSE #3		

12
9
23
5
2
10
17

FOUR

When Authority Is Abused At Your Expense

GroupSpeak: *"Submission is something that has never been easy for me; especially if I don't like the one in charge. And if I'm hurt by someone in authority, all I want to do is attack. These are hard words for me."*

Who's in Charge Here?

Someone has to be in charge. A football team with two quarterbacks on the field calling signals would result in total chaos. A company with two presidents making decisions that are diametrically opposed would lose all productivity and market shares. A nation where two leaders were continually contradicting each other would be thrust into a state of anarchy.

There is no doubt about it. Someone has to be in charge. Whether in business, at home, in school, or in the community, someone has to wear the mantle of leadership. Someone must bear the responsibility of providing primary direction.

Many who are in positions of authority are worthy of their office. They are just, kind, and reasonable. But others are not so. They rule with a heavy hand, bruising everyone they touch. Yes, someone does have to be in charge. But what happens when those who are in charge hurt you? What happens when those in charge use their position for their own gain, with no consideration of the pain you suffer? What happens when those in charge abuse their authority at your expense? The walls can close in fast when we are hurt by abusive authority. Perhaps Peter can help relieve some of the pressure.

GETTING ACQUAINTED

Testing the Limits
Take a simple test. Read each statement below. Then respond to each statement by circling either true or false.

True False Most people do not like to submit to authority.
True False Our past experiences with those in authority determine how we respond to authority now.
True False Not all authority is biblical and deserves full obedience.
True False Before we can exercise authority, we must learn to submit to authority.
True False How we exercise authority depends upon how we define submission.

Now compare your answers with others in your small group.

Authority in Profile
Read each statement below about authority. Check the response that most closely represents your position.

1. One who is in a position of authority should be like:
   a. a wolf in sheep's clothing
   b. a velvet-covered brick
   c. a sheep in wolf's clothing
   d. a strong hand with a loose grip
   e. a dove with the instincts of a hawk
   f. other ________________
2. The most important attribute for one in authority is:
   a. discernment
   b. fairness
   c. strong mindedness
   d. principledness
   e. kindness
   f. aloofness
   g. other ________________

3. Properly exercised authority makes decisions based on:
   a. the good of the many
   b. the good of the few
   c. the good of the one
   d. the good of himself
   e. the good of no one
   f. other ______________________________
4. We know someone has abused his/her authority when:
   a. someone does not like a decision that was made
   b. some benefit at the expense of others
   c. people get hurt as a result of certain actions
   d. not everyone was allowed to give input on an issue
   e. principles are elevated above relationships
   f. other ______________________________
5. The best response to authority that is exercised questionably is to:
   a. blindly go along
   b. blatantly rebel
   c. give in resentfully
   d. submit only if it is advantageous
   e. submit only when you feel like it
   f. submit only when it is absolutely necessary
   g. other ______________________________

GAINING INSIGHT

Sometimes we suffer because of the improper use of authority. Peter and his readers knew what that kind of pain was like. In addressing this all-important issue, Peter deals with several levels of authority and submission. He lays out three very important principles to help Christians respond appropriately to authority, especially when it is abused at our expense. Let's learn from him.

Submitting Because God Said So

The first principle Peter gives us is really a foundational truth upon which the following two principles are based. Read 1 Peter 2:13-17.

13Submit yourselves for the Lord's sake to every authority instituted among men: whether to the king, as the su-

preme authority, [14]or to governors, who are sent by Him to
punish those who do wrong and to commend those who
do right. [15]For it is God's will that by doing good you should
silence the ignorant talk of foolish men. [16]Live as free men,
but do not use your freedom as a cover-up for evil; live as
servants of God. [17]Show proper respect to everyone: Love
the brotherhood of believers, fear God, honor the king.

1 Peter 2:13-17

Peter says a number of things here about authority and submission. Try this exercise. Answer in one sentence: What foundational principle is Peter stating regarding the issue of authority and submission?

This foundational principle obviously has to do with being willing to submit to those in authority. According to Peter, God has ordained a certain order of authority in life. It is the Christian's responsibility to live submissively within that order. Doing so brings glory to God, and shows that we honor His authority in our lives.

Why would this be important for the Christians to whom Peter was writing?

Peter also says we should live as "free men," and "servants of God." How does exercising a submissive spirit help us show the world that we are "free men" and "servants of God"?

Note Peter's statement about showing respect to everyone (v. 17). Can a Christian who does not have a submissive spirit show proper respect for other people? Explain.

What Peter is saying here is not an altogether unfamiliar theme in the Bible. Even Jesus spoke to this issue of exercising a submissive spirit to those in authority, particularly government rulers. Read the following Scripture passages in your Bible. Each one says something specific about the way God established human authority to work, and why Christians should recognize it. Fill in the chart after reading each Scripture passage.

	How does it work?	*Why recognize it?*
1 Peter 2:13-15 Matthew 17:24-27 Romans 13:1-5 Titus 3:1-8		

Scripture obviously places a firm expectation on Christians to exercise a submissive spirit to those in authority—especially governmental authority. Think about how this applies to you.

When I read what these verses say I feel (check one):

___ obligated
___ ambivalent
___ rebellious
___ other:
___tense
___reactive
___cooperative

Because:

Submitting Apart from the Person

Peter has established a foundation for his discussion. God has established the order of authority in life. It is the believer's responsibility to respond accordingly. Using this as his basis, Peter begins to directly tackle the issue of abusive authority. Read 1 Peter 2:18-19.

[18]Slaves, submit yourselves to your masters with all respect, not only to those who are good and considerate, but also to those who are harsh. [19]For it is commendable if a man bears up under the pain of unjust suffering because he is conscious of God.

1 Peter 2:18-19

Slavery was an important part of Peter's world. It was part of the fabric of life. Unfortunately, slaves were considered pieces of property rather than persons. In many cases, they were treated no better than cattle. In speaking about slaves and masters, he is making a very important application of the principle he just presented. How are slaves to relate to their masters?

Why is it important for slaves to be submissive and respectful to even harsh masters?

It is obvious Peter is telling us that submission to authority is not based on the character of the one in charge. Our choice to render a submissive spirit is not determined by whether an authority is good, bad, or indifferent. Our choice, according to Peter, is based on our relationship with God.

In order to show that you are being conscious of God, how can you relate to a person in authority who is harsh and abusive? Make a list of ways you can demonstrate the love of Christ to someone in authority who is abusive.

Now review your list. Put a plus (+) by the action that is easiest for you. Put a minus (-) by the one that is hardest. Now think, why is this particular action so hard for you? Jot down a few thoughts and share them with your small group.

Submitting When It Really Hurts

Submitting to abusive authority can really hurt. Just the fact that God said we are supposed to does not make it any easier. Peter's third principle is an encouragement for us. Read 1 Peter 2:20-25.

20But how is it to your credit if you receive a beating for
doing wrong and endure it? But if you suffer for doing good
and you endure it, this is commendable before God. 21To
this you were called, because Christ suffered for you, leav-
ing you an example, that you should follow in His steps.
22"He committed no sin, and no deceit was found in His

**mouth." 23When they hurled their insults at Him, He did not
retaliate; when He suffered, He made no threats. Instead, He
entrusted Himself to Him who judges justly. 24He Himself bore
our sins in His body on the tree, so that we might die to sins
and live for righteousness; by His wounds you have been
healed. 25For you were like sheep going astray, but now you
have returned to the Shepherd and Overseer of your souls.**

1 Peter 2:20-25

Obviously, there is no glory or applause when we are treated poorly because of something we did. But when that is not the case, what do we do? Jesus is our example for responding to abusive authority. He too was abused by those in authority. Describe how He was treated.

Why was His treatment unjust?

How is He our example in relating to those who abuse authority at our expense?

How will the Lord minister to us when we are unjustly abused?

Review the items you listed in the previous question. Which of these gives you the greatest encouragement when authority is abused at your expense? Why?

GROWING BY DOING

Fashion a Response

The person I have contact with right now that abuses his/her authority at my expense is:

I believe this person abuses authority at my expense because:

An example I can share is:

I can demonstrate each of the principles from this Bible study in this situation in the following ways.

❑ Since exercising a submissive spirit is appropriate for recognizing God's authority in my life, I can:
❑ Because submitting to authority is not dependent upon the character of the person in authority, I will:
❑ Jesus Christ will be my example and encouragement for dealing with this person who abuses authority at my expense, because:

A Case in Point

Think of a situation in which someone abused his/her authority at your expense. Perhaps you are dealing with such a person right now. Or, maybe you have had difficulty with someone in the past. Write a brief case study about it below, citing one situation you have encountered with this individual. Share it with the group. Decide how the principles from this study can be best applied to your situation.

Can you think of any situations in which Christians *should not* submit to abusive authority? If so, explain.

Pointing Out Specifics

Dealing with someone who abuses authority at your expense will always be a matter of choice. Their treatment of you really has little to do with your response to them. Below are numerous statements from 1 Peter 2:13-25. Each statement is a concrete application of the principles Peter discusses for dealing with abusive authority. As you read the statements, check up to three that you struggle with the most.

__ submit for the Lord's sake (v. 13)
__ live as servants of God (v. 16)

__ show proper respect to everyone (v. 17)
__ it is commendable if a man bears up under the pain of unjust suffering (v. 19)
__ because he is conscious of God (v. 19)
__ to this you were called (v. 21)
__ because Christ suffered for you, leaving you an example (v. 21)
__ He did not retaliate (v. 23)
__ He made no threats (v. 23)
__ He entrusted Himself to Him who judges justly (v. 23)
__ by His wounds you have been healed (v. 24)

Now look again. Beside each statement you checked, jot a brief note explaining why you struggle with this particular item. Then note one action you can take to build each statement you checked into your response to those who abuse authority at your expense.

GOING THE SECOND MILE

Spend some time this week reflecting on how you relate to those who abuse authority at your expense. Think of a specific situation and a specific individual. What would you want God to do in your life through this situation?

What would you desire for God to do in the other person's life? In the space below, write a prayer for yourself and for the other person.

My Prayer for Myself Is

My Prayer for ______________ Is

I GET NO RESPECT!

FIVE

Enduring What You Don't Deserve

GroupSpeak: *"Keeping my witness intact is usually not my first thought when I get beat up for no reason. It's not my second thought either. In fact, it generally doesn't even enter my mind! Hmm . . . I guess I have some work to do, huh?"*

I Get No Respect!

Comedian Rodney Dangerfield has made a living out of getting no respect from people. He is always getting kicked around for something he did not do. He even gets abused for trying to do something right.

There is a little bit of Rodney in all of us. How often do you feel like you get no respect from people, that people knock you around undeservedly? But there is a difference when it happens to you and when it happens to Rodney. When it happens to him, it is funny. When it happens to us, it usually hurts.

Life isn't fair, is it? Blame and abuse come our way for no reason at all. What is worse, many times it happens when we have been consciously doing that which is good or right. Typically, the squeeze comes when we least expect it. But then again, why should we expect to suffer for right-doing? It is just not fair!

Peter knows exactly how you feel. It is not fair when you suffer for doing right. It is not fair when you are abused for doing good. So, what can you do about it? Peter has a number of suggestions.

GETTING ACQUAINTED

Animal Instincts

Think about those inner impulses you have when you suffer for doing good. Or how about your first reactions when you suffer for something you did not do? Complete each statement below by checking the appropriate response.

a. When I experience abuse and harsh treatment after doing something good, I feel like a:

____ caged panther, endlessly pacing with eyes glaring
____ playful chimpanzee, seemingly oblivious to anything
____ sly fox, looking for a fat hen to eat
____ coiled snake, ready to strike at whatever moves
____ elephant that doesn't forget
____ grizzly bear, rearing up and roaring
____ laboratory rat, forced to accept what I receive

b. When I am accused of doing something I did not do, I respond like a:

____ meek lamb, willingly led to the slaughter
____ frightened ostrich, with its head in the sand
____ strong eagle, soaring above the earth
____ little mouse, scampering to the safety of its hole
____ raging bull, challenging anything in its path
____ great shark, quietly prowling for a victim
____ sleeping dog, better to be left alone

c. When I suffer for doing good, the thing that helps me handle the hurt is to become like a:

____ chameleon, changing according to the situation
____ wild stallion, running free and unbridled
____ dove, peacefully fluttering on the wind
____ whale, blowing it all out the top
____ owl, quietly watching from a high vantage point
____ parrot, talking and talking and talking
____ sheep dog, staying faithfully at my post

GAINING INSIGHT

When we do not seem to be getting any respect, the issue of fairness tends to be our most basic consideration. We sense a need to know why. But according to Peter, the issue is whether or not we are responding in a way that is worthy of the name of Christ. Peter, as well as his readers, knew the pain of suffering in spite of doing good. Out of his experience, he gives us four very sound pieces of counsel for navigating through the hurt of unjust suffering.

Live in Harmony

The first bit of counsel Peter gives for enduring unjust treatment involves our relationships with Christians. Read 1 Peter 3:8.

[8]Finally, all of you, live in harmony with one another; be sympathetic, love as brothers, be compassionate and humble.

1 Peter 3:8

Think of what it means for something, or someone, to be in harmony. The very word *harmony* can stimulate a number of pictures in our mind. It speaks of contentment, peace, and rest. It creates images of people living together with little friction and reduced stress. What picture does the word harmony conjure up in your mind? In the space below, draw a picture of something that illustrates the kind of harmony Peter is writing about. As you draw, think about how your illustration helps you better understand the kind of relationships Peter describes.

Why would Peter give this advice to Christians who were suffering from harsh abuse and unjust treatment?

Note the qualities Peter says are present when believers are in harmony with each other. List and define each one.

Now consider, how do these various qualities build harmony between believers?

Minister God's Blessing

When someone is hurting us, the most natural thing is to strike back in self-defense, or to take the best path toward survival. Peter offers another option. Read 1 Peter 3:9-12.

**9Do not repay evil with evil or insult with insult, but with
blessing, because to this you were called so that you may
inherit a blessing. 10For, "Whoever would love life and see
good days must keep his tongue from evil and his lips
from deceitful speech. 11He must turn from evil and do
good; he must seek peace and pursue it. 12For the eyes of
the Lord are on the righteous and His ears are attentive to
their prayer, but the face of the Lord is against those who
do evil."**

1 Peter 3:9-12

Peter is giving us a tall order, isn't he? He seems to be saying that believers are called by God to minister His blessing to others, particularly to those who abuse us. Retaliation, self-vindication, and resistance are not options. Is this easy or difficult for you to do? Why?

Peter quotes from Psalm 34:12-16, which promises blessing to those who minister God's blessing to others. What promises are given here for those who do this? What kind of blessing can they look for in return?

Of all that Peter says in these verses, what is most likely to motivate you to minister God's blessing to those who abuse you? What least motivates you? Explain.

How can you minister God's blessing to those who unjustly cause you pain? List a number of specific actions.

Look over your list. Put a plus (+) next to those you already do. Put a minus (–) by those that you do not do now. Put a star (*) by those you are trying to work on. Now evaluate. How can you improve your profile as a Minister of God's Blessing?

Be a Ready Witness

It is understandable that if we do not retaliate against unjust suffering, someone might ask us why. Therefore, we should always be ready to answer. Read 1 Peter 3:13-16.

[13]Who is going to harm you if you are eager to do good?
[14]But even if you should suffer for what is right, you are
blessed. Do not fear what they fear; do not be frightened.
[15]But in your hearts set apart Christ as Lord. Always be
prepared to give an answer to everyone who asks you to
give the reason for the hope that you have. But do this
with gentleness and respect, [16]keeping a clear con-
science, so that those who speak maliciously against your
good behavior in Christ may be ashamed of their slander.

1 Peter 3:13-16

Wow, what a thought! If Jesus Christ is really Lord of our lives, then we do not need to be afraid to suffer for what is right. Preferably, that will not happen. But when it does, tremendous opportunities will be opened up to talk about it with others. What specifically are we to be ready to share with anyone who asks?

Why will this quality of hope be evident to others when we suffer for doing good?

Note how we are to share our hope with those who ask. Why is this significant?

Are you always a ready and prepared witness? Try grading yourself. Fill out the "grade card" below. Then give yourself an overall grade.

READY WITNESS REPORT CARD

	Grade	Comments
Set apart Christ as Lord		
Always prepared to answer		
Obviously hopeful outlook		
Answer with gentleness		
Answer with respect		
Answer with a clear conscience		

A=4.0 B=3.0 C=2.0 D=1.0 F=0

OVERALL GRADE: ______

Receive the Blessing of Jesus

Once again Peter refers to the sufferings of Jesus Christ as our example for handling unjust treatment. Read 1 Peter 3:17-18, 21b-22.

17It is better, if it is God's will, to suffer for doing good than
for doing evil. 18For Christ died for sins once for all, the
righteous for the unrighteous, to bring you to God. He was put to death in the body but made alive by the Spirit. . . .

1 Peter 3:17-18

21. . . by the resurrection of Jesus Christ, 22who has gone
into heaven and is at God's right hand—with angels, authorities and powers in submission to Him.

1 Peter 3:21b-22

According to Peter, enduring unjust suffering can bring great blessing. It did to Jesus. It can for us too. As you read and reflect on Peter's words, how would you describe the blessing that came to Jesus?

How does that blessing enter our experiences when we suffer for doing good?

Obviously, just knowing something does not make it personal. On the other hand, simply recognizing the blessing that is already ours can bring a tremendous amount of relief. Just think about what this blessing can mean to you personally. Draw a word picture.

Because of this great blessing, an appropriate response when I am suffering for doing good is:

- ❑ to focus my mind on . . .
- ❑ to use my mouth as . . .
- ❑ to open my heart to . . .
- ❑ to turn my hands into . . .
- ❑ to direct my feet toward . . .

GROWING BY DOING

Learning by Example

Many of God's people have suffered for doing good. The Bible is full of such examples. We can learn from these courageous saints. Read the following Bible passages. How did these people demonstrate the principles Peter gives us? How were they blessed by God? When you suffer for doing good, how can you be like them?

	What They Did	*Blessing Received*	*What I Learn*
JOSEPH Genesis 45:4-20			
DAVID 1 Samuel 26:7-25			
ELISHA 2 Kings 6:8-23			
DANIEL Daniel 6:1-23			
PAUL & SILAS Acts 16:16-34			

Making It Personal
Analyze your behavior when you suffer for doing good. Make a bar graph showing how your behavior exhibits Peter's counsel for responding to unjust treatment.

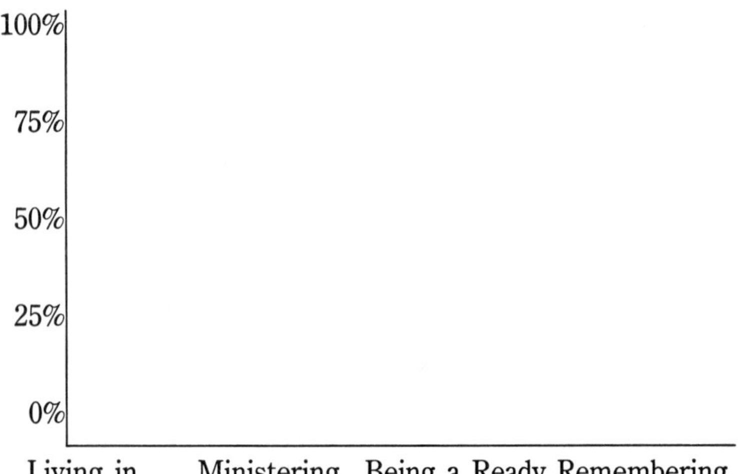

❑ Review your percentages. Which one area would you like to improve in most? Why?

❑ What will you have to do to bring your percentage up? List several specific actions.

GOING THE SECOND MILE

Many of the psalms are prayers written by those who were suffering, even though they were doing that which was right and good. Take some time this week to read the psalms listed below. Reflect on each one. Then note how you might be comforted when you are suffering for doing good.

❑ Psalm 3

❑ Psalm 5

❑ Psalm 12

❑ Psalm 26

❑ Psalm 27

❑ Psalm 55

NUMBER 2!
#2
THE DEN IS IN
#23

SIX

Waiting for It All to End

GroupSpeak: *"Waiting in a long line at K-mart is a whole lot different from waiting for something to stop hurting. How can God really expect me to occupy my time when I'm waiting for my pain to pass? That's not very realistic."*

Watching Time Go By

Waiting . . . when seconds seem like hours and hours like an eternity. Waiting is seldom fun, especially when you are hurting. Pain and suffering only compound the anxiety of waiting. We wonder what will happen next. We wonder how long we can endure. We wonder if anything good will result. But most of all, we wonder when it will all end . . . and we wait.

But as the saying goes, "A watched pot never boils." Periods of waiting, while difficult, need not be endless hours of wondering when it will all end. Indeed, periods of waiting can be very active times—times of doing something positive for other people. At least, this was Peter's perspective. Perhaps he can teach us something about *how* to wait for it all to end.

GETTING ACQUAINTED

Memorable Moments

Everyone has had experiences of waiting—at the grocery store, in the doctor's office, at the hospital waiting room.

Think of some times when you have had to wait. Share some of these memorable moments with your small group.

My Waiting Experiences

My most difficult waiting experience was . . .

My most rewarding waiting experience was . . .

The waiting experience I encounter most often is . . .

The waiting experience that I hope never happens again is . . .

My most exciting waiting experience was . . .

My most boring waiting experience was . . .

The waiting experience that really stresses me out is . . .

When in the midst of a waiting experience, how do you typically occupy your time?

While You Wait

All of us have typical "waiting postures" we assume whenever we are forced to wait for something. Think about what you do, and how you act, when you have to wait. Then answer the following questions.

What do you do while you are waiting . . .

in the doctor's office?

in a traffic jam?

in a slow moving checkout line?

for an important phone call?

for the church service to start?

at the hospital waiting room?

for the waitress to bring your meal?

for the tax refund check?

When in the midst of waiting experiences, how would you rate . . .

your stress level?
___ high ___ medium ___ low

your ability to occupy your mind with positive thoughts?
___ good ___ fair ___ poor

your interactions with other people?
___ relaxed ___ preoccupied ___ tense

your effectiveness at doing what needs to be done?
___ productive ___ lethargic ___ debilitated

GAINING INSIGHT

Peter was hurting badly; yet, he did not focus his mind on when it would all end. He already knew that it would end. In fact, the end was already near. Therefore, he set his mind on how to best use the waiting period doing the work of God's kingdom. While the walls were closing in hard and fast, Peter wanted to make time in ministry while there was still time to make. Let's see what kind of ministry Peter considers worthy of our time while we are waiting for it all to end.

The Ministry of Prayer
Even in the midst of painful difficulties, one ministry we can always discharge is that of prayer. Indeed, according to Peter, it is imperative. Read 1 Peter 4:7.

[7]The end of all things is near. Therefore, be clear minded and self-controlled so that you can pray.

1 Peter 4:7

Peter was convinced that the suffering they were experiencing meant that Jesus would soon return. While his time tables were not quite right, his concern for prayer was right on.

How about you? Is it easy or difficult for you to maintain an effective ministry of prayer during painful times? Explain.

Why do you think Peter stressed the importance of the ministry of prayer while we are waiting for our Lord?

Peter links the activity of prayer with being clear minded and self-controlled. How are these things related to prayer?

When we are in the midst of painful trials, prayer can be one of the hardest things to do. So often our pain makes our prayers seem empty and powerless. But Jesus Himself often withdrew to pray during stressful times, or prior to challenging experiences. Read the following Scripture passages.

[15]Yet the news about Him spread all the more, so that crowds of people came to hear Him and to be healed of their sicknesses. [16]But Jesus often withdrew to lonely places and prayed.

Luke 5:15-16

[1]Then Jesus told His disciples a parable to show them that they should always pray and not give up.

Luke 18:1

[24]"Until now you have not asked for anything in My name. Ask and you will receive, and your joy will be complete."

John 16:24

[24]"Therefore I tell you, whatever you ask for in prayer, believe that you have received it, and it will be yours."

Mark 11:24

7"If you remain in Me and My words remain in you, ask whatever you wish, and it will be given you."

John 15:7

26"Watch and pray so that you will not fall into temptation. The spirit is willing, but the body is weak."

Matthew 26:41

Now think, according to Jesus' words and example, what will it take for you to have an effective ministry of prayer during tough times? Circle three words that apply:

persistent	open	discerning
obedient	alert	consistent
decisive	faithful	dependent
committed	visionary	expectant
disciplined	believing	focused
guided	eager	sensitive
unhurried	patient	aware

List two things you will have to do to put these words into action:

(1)

(2)

The Ministry of Forbearance

Peter has twice spoken of the need for believers to get along with each other. But here he speaks of that process as a ministry, rather than a duty or a need. Read 1 Peter 4:8-9.

8Above all, love each other deeply, because love covers a multitude of sins. 9Offer hospitality to one another without grumbling or complaining.

1 Peter 4:8-9

Peter charges us to love each other *deeply*. The word *deeply* means to be fully stretched out, like a horse straining to run at full gallop. How does this word picture help you better understand Peter's charge to love other believers?

What kind of relationships will this kind of love produce between Christians?

What is hospitality and how does offering hospitality without grumbling or complaining relate to this practice of mutual tolerance?

List five ways you can practice this ministry of forbearing with fellow believers. Then evaluate how well you do these things.

	ALWAYS	SOMETIMES	SELDOM
(1)	___	___	___
(2)	___	___	___
(3)	___	___	___
(4)	___	___	___
(5)	___	___	___

What would help you improve in your ministry of forbearing with other Christians?

The Ministry of Service

A third area of ministry for Christians who are waiting for the end is that of service. For Peter, this service functions in very specific ways. Read 1 Peter 4:10-11.

[10]Each one should use whatever gift he has received to serve others, faithfully administering God's grace in its various forms. [11]If anyone speaks, he should do it as one speaking the very words of God. If anyone serves, he should do it with the strength God provides, so that in all things God may be praised through Jesus Christ. To Him be the glory and the power for ever and ever. Amen.

1 Peter 4:10-11

The word Peter uses for gifts is that which means "spiritual gifts"; that is, those gifts which are given by the Holy Spirit for works of service and ministry. How does Peter say that we are to use these gifts in service?

What is the goal of using our gifts?

Understanding what our spiritual gifts are, and developing them, can help us find fulfillment in the ministry of service. There are various passages in the Bible where spiritual gifts are referred to, and/or listed. Below is a compilation of the spiritual gifts listed in various passages in the Bible. Put a check mark (✓) next to those spiritual gifts you think you have. Then have your small group members affirm what spiritual gifts they see in you.

___ Service	___ Faith	___ Prophecy
___ Teaching	___ Healing	___ Exhortation
___ Encouragement	___ Apostle	___ Celibacy
___ Giving	___ Administration	___ Intercession
___ Leadership	___ Helps	___ Craftsmanship
___ Mercy	___ Evangelist	___ Discerning of Spirits
___ Wisdom	___ Pastor	___ Interpretation of Tongues
___ Knowledge	___ Hospitality	
___ Miracles	___ Tongues	

As Peter says, using our spiritual gifts in service should bring glory to God. We can assume this means it is possible to use our gifts to glorify ourselves instead. Sometimes it can be hard to tell the difference—even in ourselves. Try this exercise. List up to five questions you can ask yourself to evaluate whether you are using your spiritual gifts to glorify God or yourself. (For example, "Do I expect to be applauded after an act of service or ministry?")

___ Yes ___ No (1)

___ Yes ___ No (2)

___ Yes ___ No (3)

___ Yes ___ No (4)

___ Yes ___ No (5)

Now go back and check each question with a "Yes" or a "No," or both. How did you do? Does your ministry of service focus more on your own needs, or on God's glory? Share your results with your small group.

GROWING BY DOING

Marking Time
How well are you marking time while you wait for it all to end? Peter gives us some very good advice. Try developing your own action plan for putting his words into practice.

Regarding the ministry of prayer:

A personal strength I can build on to help me in this ministry is . . .

A weakness I need to overcome to be more effective in this ministry is . . .

Something I am already doing that will help me further develop this ministry is . . .

Something I can do to improve in this ministry is . . .

Some resources that will help me be more effective in this ministry are . . .

Regarding the ministry of forbearance:

A personal strength I can build on to help me in this ministry is . . .

A weakness I need to overcome to be more effective in this ministry is . . .

Something I am already doing that will help me further develop this ministry is . . .

Something I can do to improve in this ministry is . . .

Some resources that will help me be more effective in this ministry are . . .

Regarding the ministry of service:

A personal strength I can build on to help me in this ministry is . . .

A weakness I need to overcome to be more effective in this ministry is . . .

Something I am already doing that will help me further develop this ministry is . . .

Something I can do to improve in this ministry is . . .

Some resources that will help me be more effective in this ministry are . . .

GOING THE SECOND MILE

Spend some time this week thinking about how others have touched your life through each of these three ministries. In the space below, list a few names of those who have ministered to you through prayer, by forbearance, and in service. Then beside each name, list an act of appreciation you can do in return.

Those who have ministered to me through prayer . . .

Those who have ministered to me by forbearance . . .

Those who have ministered to me in service . . .

SEVEN

Going from Bad to Worse

GroupSpeak: *"Christians today don't really suffer for their faith, do they? At least I don't. Not that I know of, anyway. But, maybe that says something about me."*

Turning up the Heat

Out of the frying pan, into the fire! At least, that is the way our lives feel sometimes. Just about the time we adjust to one painful difficulty, something else comes along to make matters worse. Life would definitely be much easier if we only had to deal with one pain at a time. Unfortunately, life is not that neat—or simple.

We can really feel the heat when pain comes because of our faith in Jesus Christ. It is one thing to suffer from crises and tragedies that happen just because that's the way life is. But to suffer pain intentionally inflicted because we believe in Jesus Christ is oftentimes harder to take. After all, we belong to God. We serve Him. Does that not afford some shield and protection from the hostility of the world?

There may be times when you suffer because you are a Christian. How do you handle yourself when the heat gets turned up? What happens to your attitude? One of Peter's primary concerns for his people was just that: will they be able to hold up under fire?

GETTING ACQUAINTED

A Closer Look

What kind of experiences have you had with persecution? While few of us will suffer imprisonment or martyrdom, we may meet resistance in more subtle ways. Respond to each statement below.

a. WHO: The person most likely to give me grief about being a Christian is (check one):

___ my boss	___ friend
___ a coworker	___ family member
___ a neighbor	___ other: ________________

b. WHAT: When I am "attacked" because of my faith, I am (circle one from each list):

persevering	wishy-washy
confident	insecure
joyful	retaliatory
easy-going	scared
tolerant	inconsistent
loyal	reluctant
forgiving	apprehensive

c. WHEN: A time I definitely suffered for my faith was when . . .

d. WHERE: The place I am most likely to experience difficulty because of my faith (rank in order):

___ home
___ work
___ neighborhood
___ social circle
___ civic organization/club
___ other: ________________________________

e. WHY: The reason I am most likely to suffer for my faith is . . .

GAINING INSIGHT

Often, when we suffer because of our faith, it is our attitude that suffers most. To be sure, any kind of persecution will hurt, whether blatant or subtle. However, when we feel pain because of our faith, many of our inner reactions may not measure up to the faith we profess.

Peter knew such suffering. In fact, in this passage he finally addresses the issue that prompted him to write his letter; that is, suffering because of faith in Jesus. In it he gives us four check-points to evaluate how our attitudes are holding up when our faith is under fire.

From What Perspective Do You View Painful Trials? First, Peter talks about two different perspectives we can have in viewing our circumstances. Read 1 Peter 4:12-13.

[12]Dear friends, do not be surprised at the painful trial you are suffering, as though something strange were happening to you. [13]But rejoice that you participate in the sufferings of Christ, so that you may be overjoyed when His glory is revealed.

1 Peter 4:12-13

According to what Peter says, what are the two perspectives from which we can view suffering for Jesus' name?

How does our perspective affect the conclusions we draw about our difficult experiences?

Why does Peter consider it a privilege to participate in the sufferings of Christ?

How can this perspective produce a joyful attitude in suffering?

For What Reasons Do You Suffer?

In the next passage, Peter makes it clear that there are right and wrong reasons to endure suffering. We need to be able to clearly see the difference between the two. Read 1 Peter 4:14-16.

[14]If you are insulted because of the name of Christ, you
are blessed, for the Spirit of glory and of God rests on you.
[15]If you suffer, it should not be as a murderer or thief or any
other kind of criminal, or even as a meddler. [16]However, if
you suffer as a Christian, do not be ashamed, but praise
God that you bear that name.

1 Peter 4:14-16

Peter states both right and wrong reasons for suffering. List these reasons on the following chart.

RIGHT REASONS	WRONG REASONS

Why do you suppose Peter feels it is necessary to warn these Christians about suffering for the wrong reasons?

Why is suffering for the sake of Christ a blessing?

How should this shape your attitude toward the painful times when your faith is under fire?

What Is Your Future Prospect?

Once again Peter brings up the issue of judgment. Judgment is a certainty, both for the believer and the unbeliever alike. But for the Christian, judgment is both a reason for joy in suffering, and a checkpoint to evaluate his/her suffering. Read 1 Peter 4:17-18.

17For it is time for judgment to begin with the family of God; and if it begins with us, what will the outcome be for those who do not obey the gospel of God? 18And, "If it is hard for the righteous to be saved, what will become of the ungodly and the sinner?"

1 Peter 4:17-18

Peter indicates that judgment will come to both the righteous and the unrighteous. Yet, he seems to imply that these are two distinct kinds of judgment. How would you describe the difference between the judgment Christians face and that of the unbeliever?

Peter seems to be saying that people have a choice. They can experience God's judgment now as His children, and let it prepare them for their future prospect. Or, they can experience it later, as unbelievers, and remove all hope of a future prospect. How does the judgment we believers experience now prepare us for the future glory we will receive when Jesus returns?

How can this perspective of judgment bring joy into your life when you suffer for Jesus' name?

How Is Your Commitment When Your Faith Is Under Fire?

The last checkpoint Peter gives deals with our loyalties. Loyalty that is never tested is never proven. For us Christians, the true test of our loyalty will be when our faith is under fire. Read 1 Peter 4:19.

[19]So then, those who suffer according to God's will should commit themselves to their faithful Creator and continue to do good.

1 Peter 4:19

What do you think Peter means by the phrase "suffer according to God's will"?

What kind of commitment is Peter calling us to exercise?

What can we count on when we make that kind of commitment?

GROWING BY DOING

Choosing Your Joy

Obviously for Peter, enduring the hostility of unbelievers did not mean wallowing in self-pity, or adopting a martyr's complex. It involved radiating joy. How well do you maintain an attitude of joy when your faith is under fire? Choose one statement from each group that will help you maintain a joyful attitude when you suffer for being a Christian.

EIGHT

Called to Glory

GroupSpeak: *"The road really gets long sometimes—tiring too. But there's something about this 'going home to glory' that keeps it interesting, to say the least. When the pain hits hard, it all sounds too good to be true."*

Remember the Goal

Life is a journey long and hard. There is pain along the way—bumps and bruises abound. Scrapes and scratches are the norm. Darkness is abundant. The terrain can be brutal, the pain unbearable. The hurts seem endless. There are times when we wonder if we will make it. Most do. Some do not.

For the Christian, there is a special incentive to endure the journey; a reward that makes the hurt more bearable. This reward was purchased for us at a great price. It is ours. It is not only our reward, but our destination. It brings meaning into our pain and suffering. It is *eternal* glory.

But not only is there incentive, there is assistance to endure the journey as well. In these last words from Peter, we are given a number of stepping stones on which to walk as we journey toward our destination. These stepping stones can keep us sure-footed and solid as we journey along the road to our eternal glory.

GETTING ACQUAINTED

My Life Story

Everyone can give advice based on their own personal experiences. Think about the painful and difficult times in your life. What kind of advice could you give to assist others in handling their own hurtful situations? Now, write a book about it!

- ❑ The title of my book would be:
- ❑ A few chapter titles would be:
- ❑ The main emphasis of my book would be:
- ❑ Two choice illustrations I could use are:
- ❑ My bottom line, a wrap-up statement, would be:

Famous Last Words

Generally, "famous last words" are the final bits of counsel by which a person wants to be remembered. Often, they are sifted down through a lifetime of learning, and put in the briefest, most succinct form possible. What famous last words could you leave to assist others in handling the hurtful times in their lives? Jot down a few things and share them.

Let's Take a Trip

How has your journey toward glory been so far? Read each statement below and check the appropriate response.

1. My journey most often feels like a:
   a. ride in the back of a pickup truck
   b. river rafting adventure
   c. fast ride on a freeway
   d. Sunday drive along back roads
   e. vacation on an ocean cruise liner
   f. cross-country train trip

2. The weather conditions I most often encounter on my journey are:
   a. torrential downpour
   b. sunny and warm
   c. blizzard conditions
   d. mild but overcast
   e. damp and foggy
   f. light breeze
   g. threatening storm front

3. The road I feel like I am driving on most of the time is a:
   a. bumpy dirt road
   b. freshly paved highway
   c. construction zone
   d. dusty gravel road
   e. street full of potholes
   f. twisting and winding mountain road

4. The kind of vehicle I feel like I am traveling in most of the time is:
   a. the Concorde
   b. Model A
   c. rowboat
   d. dump truck
   e. tire inner tube
   f. Ferrari
   g. RV
   h. kayak

5. I feel like I spend a lot of trip time:
   a. in the repair shop
   b. waiting at the bus terminal
   c. getting bad gas mileage
   d. lost on back country roads
   e. asking directions
   g. looking at the map
   h. making good time
   i. at a rest stop

GAINING INSIGHT

Peter closes his letter as he began, with the assurance and promise of eternal glory. Because of their faith in Jesus Christ, his readers have already entered into God's Kingdom. Soon, they will enter into the glory God has prepared for them, in the presence of Jesus. But first, these last few bits of counsel are to assist them in the long journey still ahead. Most of what Peter says here he has already said. This is his final statement to draw it all together. Let's see what assistance Peter gives to help us negotiate the pitfalls and potholes in our journey to eternal glory.

The Stepping Stone of Humility

Peter has often spoken of humility in his letter. This time, however, he does not limit his words to any particular situation or category of person. Read 1 Peter 5:5b-6.

5Clothe yourselves with humility toward one another, because, "God opposes the proud but gives grace to the humble." 6Humble yourselves, therefore, under God's mighty hand, that He may lift you up in due time.

1 Peter 5:5b-6

Peter's concern is with an attitude by which God's people are to be known. Think about what Peter says. What does it mean to "clothe yourselves with humility"? Write a dictionary definition.

How does humility influence our relationships with other believers?

How does humility assist us through the painful times of our lives?

How is humility before God related to humility toward others?

How will God honor those who are truly humble before Him?

Test your own humility quotient. Circle your response to each statement below: Y = yes, N = no, S = sometimes.

I serve others in plain and ordinary ways.	Y	N	S
I recognize the worth of others.	Y	N	S
I consider others worthy of my service.	Y	N	S
I always view others as the objects of God's love.	Y	N	S
I do not consider myself better than anyone else.	Y	N	S
I place the needs of others above my own.	Y	N	S
I do not struggle when others are elevated above me.	Y	N	S
I am happy for those who gain achievements that I want.	Y	N	S

Now reflect. Which of the above statements best characterizes humility for you personally? Why?

Think about which statement above is the most difficult for you to practice. What would help you do this better?

The Stepping Stone of Dependence

The second stepping stone involves how we are to respond to God in the midst of our pain. According to Peter, the appropriate response to God is that of dependence. Read 1 Peter 5:7.

[7]Cast all your anxiety on Him because He cares for you.
1 Peter 5:7

Dependence can be a difficult thing to learn sometimes. Our culture encourages an inflated view of self-sufficiency. But when our lives become filled with anxiety because of difficult experiences, we realize just how much we need God's care. How does casting our anxiety on God demonstrate our dependence upon Him?

For what do you most need to depend on God during painful times?

Can God demonstrate His care in our lives if we do not cast our anxieties on Him? Why?

Scripture has a great deal to say about God's ability to care for us in the midst of our anxieties. One notable Scripture passage is given below. Read and reflect on what it says about God's care.

[6]Do not be anxious about anything, but in everything, by prayer and petition, with thanksgiving, present your requests to God. [7]And the peace of God, which transcends all understanding, will guard your hearts and your minds in Christ Jesus.
Philippians 4:6-7

Now, jot down some ways God's care has been demonstrated in your own life, particularly in the painful times.

How easy is it to depend on God when things get rough?

In the following list, put a check mark (√) by those items where you find it most difficult to depend on God's care.

___ When I am having financial difficulties
___ When my family relationships are not going well

___ When my job is on the line
___ When I am hurt deeply by someone I trusted
___ When someone I care about dies
___ When someone spreads malicious gossip about me
___ When I am having chronic physical problems
___ When I have reached the end of my rope emotionally
___ When I am abused by my boss and/or coworkers
___ When a family member has a handicap or disease

Based on what Peter says, and on Philippians 4:6-7, what can you do to more fully depend on God's care during your difficult experiences?

The Stepping Stone of Resistance

Peter introduces a new factor into the equation of living in the midst of pain. Awareness of the devil and his schemes during our difficult times is an important stepping stone upon which to walk. Read 1 Peter 5:8-9.

**8Be self-controlled and alert. Your enemy the devil prowls around like a roaring lion looking for someone to devour.
9Resist him, standing firm in the faith, because you know that your brothers throughout the world are undergoing the same kind of sufferings.**

1 Peter 5:8-9

What can we learn about the devil in these verses?

How are we most vulnerable to the devil during painful times? How can we respond to the devil?

Noting what Peter says in verse 9, how would you characterize the relationship between the devil and suffering?

Knowing your enemy is essential for success in any kind of battle. This is no less true of the spiritual battles we encounter with the devil. What schemes does the devil use to "devour" us during our painful times? Do a brief Scripture search. Write down what you learn about the devil's tactics.

Zechariah 3:1

Matthew 13:19

Matthew 13:38-39

John 8:44

2 Corinthians 2:10-11

2 Corinthians 11:3

Ephesians 2:1-2

Revelation 2:10

The Stepping Stone of Endurance

Endurance is Peter's last stepping stone for helping us through the pain and suffering of life. For Peter, the important thing is not *how* we endure. Neither is it *why* we should endure. Peter's interest is in *what* God does for those who do endure. Read 1 Peter 5:10-11.

[10]And the God of all grace, who called you to His eternal glory in Christ, after you have suffered a little while, will Himself restore you and make you strong, firm and steadfast. [11]To Him be the power for ever and ever. Amen.

1 Peter 5:10-11

Peter has sifted down most everything he has said about suffering into these last few words. Note . . .

> . . . how God is characterized by Peter
> . . . what God will do through our endurance

Thinking of your own difficult times, how are Peter's words significant for you personally?

The assurance and hope that Peter gives in these verses is reason to give thanks to God for His faithfulness to us. What note of thanksgiving can you give to God the next time you experience pain or suffering?

GROWING BY DOING

Finding Your Footing

What experience(s) are you having right now that is (are) particularly painful or hurtful?

How can Peter's four stepping stones give you good footing while walking through this experience?

- ❑ Humility
- ❑ Dependence
- ❑ Resistance
- ❑ Endurance

List anything that undermines your ability to find your footing on any one of these stones.

How can you deal with things that undermine your footing?

GOING THE SECOND MILE

Your study of 1 Peter is now complete. You have discussed and experienced a great deal about courage and hope in hurtful times. Based on what you have learned in these eight sessions, what can you do to live more fully in the courage and hope of Jesus Christ?

DEAR SMALL GROUP LEADER:

Picture Yourself As A Leader.

List some words that describe what would excite you or scare you as a leader of your small group.

A Leader Is Not . . .

- ❑ a person with all the answers.
- ❑ responsible for everyone having a good time.
- ❑ someone who does all the talking.
- ❑ likely to do everything perfectly.

A Leader Is . . .

- ❑ someone who encourages and enables group members to discover insights and build relationships.
- ❑ a person who helps others meet their goals, enabling the group to fulfill its purpose.
- ❑ a protector to keep members from being attacked or taken advantage of.
- ❑ the person who structures group time and plans ahead.
- ❑ the facilitator who stimulates relationships and participation by asking questions.
- ❑ an affirmer, encourager, challenger.

- ❑ enthusiastic about the small group, about God's Word, about discovering and growing.

What Is Important To Small Group Members?

- ❑ A leader who cares about them.
- ❑ Building relationships with other members.
- ❑ Seeing themselves grow.
- ❑ Belonging and having a place in the group.
- ❑ Feeling safe while being challenged.
- ❑ Having their reasons for joining a group fulfilled.

What Do You Do . . .

If nobody talks—

- ❑ Wait—show the group members you expect them to answer
- ❑ Rephrase a question—give them time to think.
- ❑ Divide into subgroups so all participate.

If somebody talks too much—

- ❑ Avoid eye contact with him or her.
- ❑ Sit beside the person next time. It will be harder for him o to talk sitting by the leader.
- ❑ Suggest, "Let's hear from someone else."
- ❑ Interrupt with, "Great! Anybody else?"

If people don't know the Bible—

- ❑ Print out the passage in the same translation and hand it o save time searching for a passage.
- ❑ Use the same Bible versions and give page numbers.
- ❑ Ask enablers to sit next to those who may need encou ment in sharing.
- ❑ Begin using this book to teach them how to study; affirm efforts.

If you have a difficult individual—

- ❑ Take control to protect the group, but recognize that expl differences can be a learning experience.
- ❑ Sit next to that person.
- ❑ To avoid getting sidetracked or to protect another g member, you may need to interrupt, saying, "Not all of u that way."
- ❑ Pray for that person before the group meeting.

ONE

Seeing Hope Through the Hurt

Our world is characterized by hopelessness, and for good reason. Our world is without Christ. And without Christ there is no hope. Hope is a distinctively Christian term. Yet, many Christians tend to live without a sense of hope, particularly when going through times of pain and suffering.

Peter has a great message in this passage. In spite of all the hurt we experience, there is hope in Jesus Christ—hope that gives us courage to face the painful times. Through the salvation God has provided for us in Jesus Christ, we have an anchor, especially in the difficult times. There are several things Peter teaches us about seeing our hope through our hurt, when everything seems hopeless.

As **Group Leader,** *you* have a choice as to which elements best fit your group, your style of leadership, and your purposes. After you examine the **Session Objectives**, select the activities under each heading with which to begin your community building.

SESSION OBJECTIVES

- √ Describe the kind of people who have hope in the midst of suffering and painful circumstances.
- √ Analyze the content of the believer's hope in Jesus Christ.
- √ Define positive ways to respond to hope in Jesus Christ while experiencing troubled times.
- √ Evaluate how this hope influences our perspective of difficult times.

Pocket Principle

1 Group members can heighten their interest and motivation by willingly submitting to a mutually agreed upon set of expectations. Knowing what is expected sets a course for the group, and frees group members to channel their energies into group life.

GETTING ACQUAINTED 20–25 minutes

Have a group member read aloud **Tough Times and Tough People.** Then choose one (or more) of the following activities to help create a comfortable, nonthreatening atmosphere.

Crossing Words
Divide the group into work teams of three to four people. Instruct each team to complete the first part of the activity in their books. After about five to eight minutes, call time and have each team share their crossword puzzles with the rest of the group. After each team has shared, direct them to do the second part of the activity. After five to eight minutes, have teams share their sentences with the rest of the group.

Conclude this time by asking: **Of the words or phrases your team listed, which one best defines *hope* for you right now?** After a brief time of reflection and sharing, move into your study.

GAINING INSIGHT 30–35 minutes

Indeed, there is not much hope in the world, is there? While those who know Jesus personally have hope, the rest of the world exists in hopelessness. After all, without Jesus, the world is hopelessly lost. Sometimes, however, even Christians can be infected with the hopelessness of the world. The hurtful experiences we have can confuse that sense of hope. Yet, in the midst of hurt, it is possible to have hope.

This first study about *hope* is pivotal to everything else Peter wants to teach us about enduring the painful times in our lives. In fact, much of what he says here will be repeated elsewhere in varying ways. That is how important this information is to Peter. Let's see what he has to say.

People Who Have Hope

Comment: **We live in a tough world. Peter's readers lived in a tough world as well. Yet, they were hopeful. Before we can have hope, we need to be the kind of people for whom hope can be real.** Have the group read 1 Peter 1:1-2, paying particular attention to the words or phrases that describe the people to whom Peter wrote.

Ask: **What words or phrases did you note that could give us a clue about what Peter's readers were experiencing?** (Peter refers to his readers as *aliens* and *scattered.* Peter was writing to people who had been displaced from their homes because of a campaign of intense and savage persecution by the Roman state. In 64 A.D. a great fire swept through Rome. Nero, the Roman Emperor, was blamed for the tragedy. He had a great passion for building. Reportedly, he desired to rebuild Rome. Then came the fire. The people were outraged. In order to divert suspicion from himself, Nero blamed the Christians. A great campaign of persecution of Christians was launched. This first letter of Peter was written immediately following the first wave of persecution.)

Ask: **Why does Peter refer to his readers as *chosen*?** (To be *chosen* means to be selected especially by God for His special purposes, through faith in Jesus Christ. It is a designation of privilege, and of status. They were people who were chosen by God, and therefore were called by His name. They belonged to no one else but Him. They lived according to His special purposes. They enjoyed the great benefits of His grace and mercy because of the status of this special relationship with God.)

Ask group members to share a time when they were each chosen by someone for something special. Encourage them to focus on the feelings they had in that particular circumstance. Allow for a brief period of sharing. Note that all of these same feelings can be enjoyed by believers, because God has especially chosen each one of us, just as He chose each of Peter's readers.

Indicate that Peter also refers to his readers as *strangers* and *scattered.* Ask: **In what ways do these terms apply to Peter's readers?** (They were forced to save their lives by fleeing from their homes. As a result, they lived in places foreign to them. However, on a deeper level, the persecution they experienced should have reminded them that their loyalties did indeed belong to another Kingdom, and a different King. As they were not citizens of the land in which they lived, so they were not citizens of the world at all. They were citizens of God's Kingdom, and to Him their allegiance belonged.)

Let your group explore this concept of *strangers in the world.* Lead them through the Scripture Search, instructing them to write a brief summary of what each passage teaches about the hope we believers have because we are strangers in this world. Do only one passage at a time. Have them write and share their summary for each passage in turn.

Ask: **How should these truths of being chosen and strangers make us feel about ourselves when the walls start closing in on us?** (It is not unusual to feel disoriented, confused, and unsure of ourselves during painful times. Knowing that we belong to God as His special people, that we are part of a glorious Kingdom beyond this world, can give us a firm anchor in hopeful thinking. We can know that God's purposes are rooted in who we are in Him, rather than in what we experience in our lives now. We can walk obediently with Jesus, because that is God's purpose for us. Even in the midst of the difficult times in life, we are in God's hands.)

Reasons Why Hope Is Real

Note that *hope* for the Christian is rooted in something beyond ourselves. It is more than just being chosen by God. While God chose us in Jesus Christ, He also took steps to make our hope alive through the eternal salvation available in Jesus Christ. Because our salvation is eternal, our hope is eternal. According to Peter, it is this eternal nature of our hope that makes it a *living hope.* Have the group read 1 Peter 1:3-5, 10-12.

Lead the group to list the points Peter makes regarding our salvation in Jesus Christ. Your list should include some of the following:

- ❑ It was extended to us on account of God's great mercy.
- ❑ Through it we have new birth by the resurrection of Jesus.
- ❑ It involves an inheritance that is indestructible.
- ❑ Our salvation is eternal and is kept in heaven for us by God's power until Jesus returns.
- ❑ It will be brought to completion when Jesus is revealed.
- ❑ The prophets were directed to prophesy about Jesus for our benefit.
- ❑ It was preached to us by those empowered by the Holy Spirit.
- ❑ The angels deeply desire to know what we have experienced.

Note that Peter gives a very comprehensive picture about this great eternal salvation we have in Jesus Christ. Tell the group to review the list. Ask: **On what specifically is our salvation based?** (The sufferings, death, and resurrection of Jesus, because of God's great mercy.)

Ask the group to listen as you once again read verses 10-12. Comment on how great we should feel because of what Peter says. The prophets who spoke thousands of years ago were speaking for our benefit. The angels intensely desire to know of the salvation we have experienced. Direct the group to circle three feeling words from the list in their books. Allow group members to share the words they chose without feeling hurried or pressured.

Ask: **How can looking at all that Peter says about our salvation give you a sense of hope in the midst of hurtful times?** (Our hope goes beyond our hurt. While our hurts are physical and tied to the physical world, our hope is eternal and is based on our eternal salvation. Nothing we experience, no matter how severe the pain, can negate the living hope we have in Jesus Christ.)

What Hope Can Do

Comment: **Our hope is a living hope, kept for us by God's power. No amount of pain we encounter on earth can take it from us. This gives us a special perspective from which to view the hard times we experience in life now.** Read 1 Peter 1:6-9. Ask: **How should your hope in Christ impact your perspective of what you experience in your life now?** (Having a living hope does not produce a pie-in-the-sky naiveté that is oblivious to reality. Having a living hope does not mean denying the presence of pain and grief in life. Rather, having such a glorious hope shapes our perspective. Because of our hope we can look beyond this present life, which is temporary, to the permanence of all that awaits us in Jesus Christ. Additionally, it is actually through the pain of our present trials that our hope in Christ is proven. Our pain is not the end. It is the proof of what God has secured for us in Jesus Christ. We can endure most any hardship when we have something for which to look forward. And in Jesus Christ, we have everything to look forward to.)

Ask: **What is God's purpose in allowing pain and hurt to enter your life?** (Painful times are allowed by God, not to hurt us, but to help us become what He wants us to be. Few things can mold our spiritual character like pain and suffering. For, no matter how great our pain, God's grace can match it. God does not mean suffering to sap our strength, but to multiply our strength for His praise. The more we see God's grace in our pain, the more we are freed to see God's glory being brought about through it.)

Ask: **How does God's purpose (in verse 8) relate to the goal of our faith that Peter talks about in verse 9?** (The more God's grace and glory are multiplied in our suffering, the more our salvation is confirmed within us as He continues to work His purposes through our pain.)

Ask: **What can you learn from verses 6-9 to help you cope with the hurt you may be experiencing in your life now?** Do not try to force or hurry sharing. Group members may need some time to reflect. Set an example by sharing something first. This will give others a chance to collect their thoughts.

GROWING BY DOING 20–25 minutes

Discovering Your Hope
Complete the creative writing exercise as directed in the book. Have each group member work individually. After about five minutes, have each group member share what they have written with the whole group. Allow the group to freely comment and question each other about what they have written.

Divide into prayer teams of three to four. Instruct group members to share one thing from their writing exercise for which they would like prayer support from the group. Each team should then pray together.

Optional—Having a Hopeful Outlook
Complete the fill-in-the-blank exercise as directed in the book. When each person is finished, ask group members to freely share what they have written. Note similarities and differences. Ask questions for clarification when appropriate.

Close with a fill-in-the-blank prayer exercise. Each group member should pray in the following manner:

❑ "One thing about hope I am thankful for is. . . ."
❑ "Help me to always remember that. . . . "

GOING THE SECOND MILE 5 minutes

Remind your group of the privilege Christians have to participate in such a glorious hope. Along with that privilege comes the responsibility to share it. Challenge them to take the time during the next week to be *sharers of hope* to someone else by completing the exercise in their books.

GROWING AS A LEADER

The setting of a small group can help you achieve more in Bible exploration and application than in a larger, more church-centered environment. As you prepare to lead this series of studies, think about the following benefits of small group Bible study. As you lead each session, try to be aware of how these benefits are being realized within your group.

- ❑ It develops good study skills by encouraging personal study, and by providing a model for serious Bible study.
- ❑ It provides a supportive environment for sharing personal responses to God's Word and challenging people to accountability.
- ❑ It offers a setting and opportunity for developing people for leadership and service, through the equipping power of the Scriptures.

TWO

Staying Clean When Things Get Dirty

When you help people who have just experienced a severe crisis, their response of gratitude can be overwhelming. In some cases, they outdo themselves in repaying the kindness and mercy you showed them. According to Peter, that should be the Christian's response to God.

In the first session, Peter's words rang with joy because of the glorious hope we have in Jesus Christ. In this session he tells us what our appropriate response should be to God. Living a clean life, Peter says, is the only response worthy of the great hope we share in Jesus Christ. But, clean living is not something we do out of a sense of responsibility, obligation, or duty. We are called to live clean lives out of joyful gratitude for our salvation.

These are indeed important words for people who were under the pressure of pain. But Peter's message in this session is clear—when things get dirty, Christians are to stay clean. Let's look at what he advises.

As **Group Leader,** *you* have a choice as to which elements best fit your group, your style of leadership, and your purposes. After you examine the **Session Objectives,** select the activities under each heading with which to begin your community building.

SESSION OBJECTIVES

√ Discuss the process by which believers can stay clean in a dirty world.
√ Analyze the central issues involved in staying clean during the difficult times.
√ Define specific actions we can take to open ourselves up to God's purifying work.

GETTING ACQUAINTED 20–25 minutes

Have a group member read aloud **Living Above It All.** Then choose one or more of the following activities to help create a comfortable, nonthreatening atmosphere.

Which Is Worse?
Instruct the group to work through the exercise in their books. When they are finished, divide the group into teams of three or four to share their responses. Then gather together and discuss the following questions before moving on with your study.

❑ **Why did you rank your number one item as number one?**
❑ **Are there any items on the list that you would classify as bad, but not necessarily wrong? Explain.**
❑ **Are there other problems that you would add to this list? Where would you put them (it) in your ranking?**
❑ **Are there any items on the list that you have had an encounter with, personally or through someone else, that you are free to share?**

GAINING INSIGHT 30–35 minutes

Comment: **Remember the saying, "You can't walk through smoke without smelling like it"? Well, living in a dirty world is much the same. It can be tough for Christians to live in our world without smelling like it now and again. But Peter is confident there is a way to stay clean when things around you get dirty. You might call it preventative**

medicine. It is not, however, like castor oil. It is a medicine we should be happy to take because of our glorious hope in Jesus Christ. That is why he begins verse 13 of chapter 1 with the word *Therefore*. In other words, everything he is about to say is a logical step from what he has just said. So let's take that step with him.

Developing Mental Discipline

Comment: **The first part of Peter's prescription has to do with our minds.** Read 1 Peter 1:13. Point out the background for the phrase "prepare your minds for action." Ask: **Do you agree or disagree with Peter's assessment that mental discipline takes work? Why or why not?** (There are so many sources of bad thinking in our world today. We are constantly bombarded by the media in various ways every day. Additionally, many Christians work in environments that are downright filthy! It can be difficult to keep your mind on the right track when so much around you is pushing you otherwise.)

Ask: **How are having a disciplined mind and staying clean in a dirty world related?** (Everything we read, see, or hear is stored in our subconscious mind. At any given point these bits of information can impact the way we think, act, or make decisions. Just like a computer, if we program our mind with garbage, eventually that is what will come out. Our minds must be clean if our behavior is to be clean.)

Lead group members through the checklist exercise. Have them check the three things that are most likely to have an impact on the way they think. Ask members to share what they checked with the rest of the group. Be alert to ask for specific examples where appropriate. Continue with the evaluation exercise as directed.

Note that Peter draws a correlation between mental discipline and focusing our attention on the hope of Jesus Christ. Ask: **How are these two ideas related?** (When we become flabby in the way we think about God, our minds become open to entertain all kinds of spiritually distracting thoughts. For Christians, maintaining the mental discipline of necessity means centering our minds on the hope we have received in Jesus

Christ. When we are so focused, we are less likely to be distracted. We can think clearly in relation to the things of God.)

Ask the group to list some ways Christians can overcome the negative influences that challenge their mental discipline. Allow for a brief time of open discussion and sharing.

Practicing Obedience

Comment: **We practice obedience in order to live above the dirt and filth in the world around us. According to Peter, obedience involves both practicing positive actions and avoiding negative actions.** Read 1 Peter 1:14-16 and 4:1-3.

Have the group analyze what it means to be obedient by filling in the chart in their books. Summarize by commenting: **Being a child of obedience means pursuing the holiness of God. Consequently, it also involves not being driven by the desires we had before we were aware of the way God wants us to live.**

Ask: **How should the nature of God influence the way we live?** (We tend to take on characteristics of the people we know and spend time with. Peter indicates that our holiness is a result of our relationship with God. We know Him. We are His children. We should bear His likeness. In human terms, it is a matter of living up to the family name. God is a holy God. We are called to reflect that same character.)

Help your group understand what holiness means. The word *holy* that Peter uses means to be separated from, to be distinct and different. Just as God is separate from, different than, and distinct in His character, so we are to be. To walk in the holiness of God, obedience is absolutely fundamental.

Ask: **What was Christ's attitude toward suffering?** Encourage group members to share their answers. Then ask: **What does it mean to arm yourself with Christ's attitude?** Let group members discuss their answers.

Encourage your group to complete the application and sharing exercise as directed in their books. Encourage them to list at least one area where their obedience to God is challenged on occasion. Listing one thing is enough for the purpose of sharing. Asking them to list any more than that may be too threatening for some. Focus your sharing on the appropriate response part of the activity. Doing so will help make this a positive activity, rather than a negative one.

Recognize the Judgment of God
Note that while God's judgment can sometimes be a threatening concept, even for Christians, it really does not need to be such a negative thing. Peter approaches the issue from a very positive perspective, making it a very practical consideration for living a clean life in a dirty world. Read 1 Peter 1:17.

Ask: **In relation to His own children, what kind of judge is God?** (Peter says that while God judges us impartially, He also judges us as our father. As a father, God is loving, caring, and concerned for our best welfare. His work of judgment in the life of a believer serves that end. He is not interested in punishing His children. His concern is for growth.)

Share with the group that the word *judge* is in the present tense, which refers to a continual process of judgment taking place within the life of the believer. The word itself means to put someone to the test in order to approve the good that is within that person. This is how God judges His children. It is not a matter of constantly looking over your shoulder. It is a continual process of making us whole for His purposes.

Ask: **How does the idea of being strangers in the world relate to the idea of God judging our lives?** (As believers, while we live on planet earth, our permanent home is God's kingdom. Hence, while we live here, we serve the purposes of our Heavenly King. Our lives will always be subject to the dictates of His judgment. Therefore, we should always walk in reverence to our Heavenly King, with the awareness that He is continually working in our lives to approve the holiness of our character.)

Live As One Redeemed
Note that Peter's last word about staying clean in a dirty world has to do with the cost of our salvation. Read 1 Peter 1:18-21. Have the group list the points Peter makes about our salvation in Jesus Christ. Your list should include some of the following:

- ❑ We were redeemed from an empty way of life.
- ❑ The cost of our salvation was the very blood of Jesus Christ, which is more precious than silver or gold.
- ❑ Jesus was the only perfect sacrifice for our sin.
- ❑ Our salvation was planned by God before the foundation of the world.
- ❑ Jesus was raised from the dead and glorified in heaven by the power of God.
- ❑ Through Jesus we are able to believe in God.
- ❑ Our faith and hope are anchored firmly in God Himself.

Ask: **What was Jesus' role in this process?** (Jesus freely gave His own life so that we could be brought back to God. He was prepared by God before the creation of the world to bring about our redemption. Because Jesus was raised from the dead and exalted in heaven, we can come to God in faith and hope.)

Comment: **Peter is attempting to help us understand what it cost God to free us from sin and make us His own.** Ask: **How should this affect the way we each live? What does this mean for you?** Allow for a brief time of reflection and sharing. Then comment: **There is no greater motivation for responding to God than this. It is almost inconceivable that God should desire to pay the ultimate price for our redemption. This becomes a challenge for us. Do we live as people who have been redeemed at such a great cost? According to Peter, the most grateful response we can make is to stay clean when things get dirty.**

GROWING BY DOING 20–25 minutes

Raising the Stakes

Divide the group into teams of three to four people. Direct group members to first complete the commitment exercise by writing down one commitment for each principle listed in their books. Each team should then spend time sharing among themselves what they have written. Request each team to spend time praying for each other before closing.

GOING THE SECOND MILE 5 minutes

Encourage group members to keep their new commitments foremost in their thinking throughout the next week. Remind them to complete the **Going the Second Mile** section at home to give themselves some added encouragement.

GROWING AS A LEADER

One of the most important roles of a small group leader is to select and develop a leader-in-training. Each small group leader should make it his or her goal to train at least one new leader each time they assume leadership for a new small group. Many leaders do not do this simply because they do not feel adequate for the task.

Nevertheless, the small group setting provides the perfect context for developing new leaders. A leader-in-training can gain hands-on experience, learn by observing another leader in action, and experience the support of the small group when he/she begins to test his/her newly developed skills.

There is a very simple process for training new leaders.

1. You, as small group leader, should take the initiative to pinpoint someone in your group who has the potential to lead a small group.
2. Talk to this person privately about his/her possible interest.
3. Have this person spend time with you as you prepare your session plans. Talk through the session with him/her. Solicit this person's feedback about the session activities.
4. After the leader-in-training has observed a few sessions, give him/her various parts of the session to lead. Vary the assignment so as to give him/her a broad exposure to all the functions of your small group.
5. Help this person plan a session to lead on his/her own. Be ready to give assistance during the session, but do not be quick to interfere. Remember, this person's style of leadership will probably be different from your own.
6. Meet with the leader-in-training afterward to evaluate. After a period of time, encourage this person to form his/her own small group.

THREE

Becoming the Person God Is Making You

What more can happen? What is the purpose of all of this? What is God thinking of? What did I do to deserve this? What am I going to do? What does God expect me to learn?

Have you ever heard yourself asking any of these questions when life started to hurt? Most of us have. Actually, these are very common questions, any one of which expresses the desire of a hurting heart to bring order to the inner chaos that pain can cause.

These questions, however, really fall short of the central issue involved in painful circumstances. None of these questions gives us the focus God wants us to have when life hurts.

So, what is the right question? When the walls start closing in, the best question to ask is *What kind of person does God want me to become?* Any other question tends to focus on trying to understand the "why" of our circumstances. But attempting to discern what kind of person God wants you to become is a more appropriate response because through your tough times, God wants to make you into His kind of person so you can do His kind of living.

As **Group Leader,** *you* have a choice as to which elements best fit your group, your style of leadership, and your purposes. After you examine the **Session Objectives**, select the activities under each heading with which to begin your community building.

SESSION OBJECTIVES

√ List and discuss the character qualities God desires to build into us during painful times.
√ Identify specific actions that keep us from becoming the person into which God wants to make us.
√ Evaluate how well our lives exhibit the particular qualities outlined in the passage.
√ Develop a strategy for building these character qualities into our walk with God.

GETTING ACQUAINTED 10–15 minutes

Have a group member read aloud **Your Kind of People.** Then choose one or more of the following activities to help create a comfortable, nonthreatening atmosphere.

Pocket Principle

1 Some small group leaders assume that the best personal sharing is stimulated either by asking deeply personal questions, or through highly introspective exercises. Many times, however, some of the best sharing happens during the lighter, more fun types of activities. The more relaxed group members are, the more they tend to reveal about themselves.

The Ideal You

Divide group members into work teams of three to four to fill in the blanks and share their responses. After teams have had ample time to share, call the group together and ask: **How did you do? How much of what you wrote would you really like to make happen in your life? Why or why not?** Finish by discussing the question in the book: **How**

does this "ideal you" stack up to the kind of person you believe God wants to make you into right now?

GAINING INSIGHT 40–45 minutes

Pocket Principle

2 **A small group leader is not the Shell Answer Man. Do not rush in to give all the answers to every question. Draw on the wisdom and knowledge of the group.**

Comment: **It is interesting to note that thus far, Peter has not dealt with the "why" of suffering. His readers had experienced intense circumstances—physical pain and abuse, false accusation, imprisonment, flight from their homes and families. Yet, Peter's focus has been on how to be a Christian in the midst of the pain. This session continues that focus. In fact, Peter writes as if he is directly addressing the question, "What kind of person does God want me to become when the walls start closing in?" Let's see what Peter's answer is.**

Loving People

Read 1 Peter 1:22–2:1. Be sure group members understand the difference between the two words Peter uses for love. Ask: **How is Peter telling us to love each other?** (Peter is making a basic distinction between liking someone, and deliberately choosing to love someone by seeking their best welfare regardless of any personal likes or preferences. In other words, he is challenging us to go beyond a mere fondness or simple appreciation for each other. He wants us to love each other as God does.)

Ask: **What is the basis for this kind of love between Christians?** (It is a love that is based solely on God, and what He has done in us through Jesus Christ. God's work in us brings us into a new family. We should, therefore, express His kind of love toward the "new relatives" we have in Jesus Christ. We are to love one another because we are related to each other.)

Lead the group to list the five barriers to love that Peter gives. Note that Peter's words are strong. To *rid yourself* means to literally put them off, cast them aside, have nothing to do with these attitudes and behaviors that destroy love between Christians. Help the group list reasons why these various attitudes/behaviors are barriers to love. It is not necessary to be exhaustive. Entertain a few responses, then move on to the next one. Share the following information about each item as appropriate:

Malice = active ill will, or a vicious nature bent on doing harm to others.

Deceit = outwardly playing a part that is acceptable, but inwardly serving the interests of your own reputation or material advantage.

Hypocrisy = acting a part; one who assumes the mannerisms, speech, and character of someone else, hiding his/her true identity.

Envy = wanting what others have, because the concern for your own status or position is greater than the concern for the welfare of others.

Slander = backbiting; gossip; speaking against another who is not there to defend him or herself, with the specific intent of defaming or harming this person's reputation.

Lead the group through the creative writing exercise. Assist group members by suggesting they draw on the listing exercise they just completed. After several minutes, call time and ask for volunteers to share what they have written.

Growing Babies

Ask: **What does it mean to be *childish*?** Entertain a few responses, then comment: **While childishness is not a very attractive character quality—even in many children—there is a specific childlike quality that Christians are to imitate.** Read 1 Peter 2:2-3.

Ask: **Why do you suppose Peter likens Christians to newborn babies?** Let your group draw a number of comparisons, then suggest that there is a sense in which Christians are always to be like babies. Babies need to be provided constant nourishment if they are to survive, grow up, and be healthy and strong. They are totally dependent on another source for their sustenance and care. Most newborn babies, especially if they are healthy, have an enormous appetite. All of these qualities Christians should possess, if they desire to be healthy and growing.

Note the particular words Peter uses, *crave pure spiritual milk.* Ask: **What does Peter mean by these words?** *(Crave* means to let your appetite be so enormous that you cannot chew or digest all that you take in. *Pure spiritual milk* refers to the nourishment that can only come from God, through His Word, and through the constantly growing relationship we have with Him. Put together, the phrase refers to the kind of person who has tasted of the good things God has given and has an enormously insatiable desire for more.)

Ask: **Why should Christians have such a big spiritual appetite?** (It is inconceivable that we would let a child constantly spoil his/her appetite with junk food. It is even more inconceivable to let a newborn baby starve. If children do not gain proper nourishment, they do not grow up properly. Potential abnormalities can occur. If Christians deprive themselves of proper spiritual nourishment, they too will cease to be healthy or spiritually normal. They can even become childish, troubled, or troublesome! A healthy baby is a hungry baby. A healthy Christian is a Christian with a continually expressed need to feed on the things of God.)

Living Stones

Read 1 Peter 2:4-8. Ask: **What point is Peter making about Jesus? Can you paraphrase what he is telling us?** (Jesus was ordained by God to be the foundation of His Church. This very stone that many have rejected, we have received. Like Him, we are now living stones in a spiritual house, being built upon Jesus Christ. He Himself is the chief cornerstone upon whom this house is established, and through whom it holds together.)

Note the three phrases Peter uses to describe believers: spiritual house, holy priesthood, offering spiritual sacrifices. Ask the group to reflect on what each phrase means. Then invite group members to share the ideas or images that each phrase brings to mind. Some of the discussion can include:

Spiritual House:

a. **Like the earthly Temple, our fellowship together is a physical demonstration of the presence and glory of God among us.**
b. **It is also a living testimony and witness of the one chief cornerstone upon which our house is being built.**
c. **As this house is being built, we are joined together in unity for His glory.**

Holy Priesthood: In the Temple, the priest served to minister the Spirit and presence of God to the people. Through Jesus Christ, all believers are charged with the task of ministering the Spirit and presence of God to fellow believers.

Offer Spiritual Sacrifices: The priest was to represent the people before God, presenting to Him the people's offerings and sacrifices. As a Holy Priesthood, all believers are called upon to bring offerings and sacrifices before God that are worthy of our calling in Jesus Christ. (For further elaboration on this phrase, suggest that the group look at Romans 12:1-2 and Hebrews 13:15-16.)

Direct group members to complete the evaluation exercise. Ask volunteers to share where they see themselves in relation to each image. Then ask: **What one thing could you do to raise any low rating you may have had in one of these three areas?** Allow for a brief time of sharing.

Testifying Witnesses

Read 1 Peter 2:9-10. Once again, note the various images Peter uses to describe the new life we have in Jesus. Ask: **What do these phrases tell us about the relationship we have with Jesus Christ, and with each other?** (Through Jesus Christ, we belong to God. We are distinct from all other people. We share in a special relationship with God and have been set apart for His purposes. As far as God is concerned, we are very important people, for whom He has reserved the best!)

Mention that all Christians have been brought out of darkness. No matter what our life was like before we met Jesus personally, we were without His light. For some that transformation was more dramatic than for others. But each transformation is of equal value to God. Invite group members to share about the personal darkness out of which God may have brought them, and how it happened.

Ask: **Why has God done all of this for us?** (God's purpose in creating a chosen people is for us to declare His goodness to the world around us. We are to be a people who give public testimony and witness to the goodness of God among us.)

Lead the group through the "declare the praises" listing exercise in their books. Through your discussion, help the group understand that living a life that declares the praises of God need not be a complicated or threatening thing. It can be as simple as reflecting a hopeful attitude, or demonstrating a sincere desire to help someone, or stopping to listen when someone needs to talk.

Distinctive Saints

Comment: **Peter tells us, once again, that because this world is not our home, we are to live a distinctive kind of life.** Read 1 Peter 2:11-12.

Ask: **What kind of life are believers called to live?** (We are not to be ruled by sinful desires. Such desires are reflective of the way the rest of the world lives. Living according to such desires means to be controlled by the power of sin, the only goal of which is to destroy our souls. Living a distinctive life before the world means first living a distinctive life within ourselves; i.e., living a life that is controlled by the Spirit of God, rather than by desires that cause spiritual compromise and deterioration.)

Ask: **What reason(s) does Peter give for Christians to be such distinctive people?** (Peter indicates that if Christians will live such obviously good lives, those who accuse them of inappropriate behavior will be discredited and put to shame. Remember, Peter's readers have already been accused of setting fire to Rome. Additionally, in Peter's time Christians were accused of treason, cannibalism, incest, and generally hating mankind. Hence, Peter tells Christians to expend their energies living good lives and doing good deeds, so as to disprove the slanderous charges and allegations made against them. Christians are to lead good lives on behalf of the welfare of the pagans who, witnessing the testimony of the Christians, may glorify God themselves.)

Comment: **It is easy to lose our distinctiveness as Christians. In an effort to be relevant, we may blend in a little too much with society at large. Often it is not in the major, black-and-white issues where believers lose their edge. Usually it is in the more subtle places, the gray areas, where we can lose our distinctiveness.** Lead the group through the "gray area" exercise in their books. Invite group members to voluntarily share and discuss their responses.

GROWING BY DOING 20–25 minutes

What Kind of Person Am I Becoming?
Divide into teams of three to four to complete this exercise. Instruct teams to first work through the performance evaluation section, and share responses with each other. Then ask group members to finish the remaining two parts of the exercise, sharing their responses together. Each team should conclude with a circle prayer activity, with each one praying for the person on their right according to what each one shared.

GOING THE SECOND MILE 5 minutes

Indicate to the group that the strength of a plan is in acting on it. Sometimes that means clearing the way so the plan can be put into effect. The **Going the Second Mile** activity will help them clear the way to put their "growth response plan" into action. Remind them to spend some time during the week completing the exercise on their own.

GROWING AS A LEADER

In any group of people there will be differences. Where there are differences, there will be disagreements. And where there are disagreements, there will be conflict. Conflict happens in every small group. It happens in varying ways and with varying degrees of intensity—from a friendly disagreement to a sharp dispute. Generally, most of us dislike conflict. It scares us. We do not always know how to respond. We are afraid of what it will do. We do not like to see people hurt. Confrontation makes us uneasy, especially when it puts us on the hot seat. Even the very word *conflict* sounds so negative.

However, conflict need not be considered a bad thing. While occasionally a small group will encounter a conflict that threatens to tear the group apart, the conflicts most groups face can be resolved with patience, kindness, mutual commitment to each other, and direct dialogue. In fact, the group will benefit from learning to deal with differences.

- ❑ Conflict can bring freshness into a stale group, and move it out of its rut.
- ❑ Conflict can help group members develop new patterns of communication.
- ❑ Conflict can stimulate creative thought, and help people think about things in new ways.
- ❑ Conflict can create a deeper understanding of yourself and others.
- ❑ Conflict can deepen relational bonds and build greater group unity.

The next time your group has a conflict, think about the benefits the group can experience. Then work for resolution toward that end.

FOUR

When Authority Is Abused At Your Expense

Few issues in the Christian life are as clear yet complex, practical yet uncomfortable, difficult to accept yet easily discussed, as the issue of submission and authority. In every area of our lives the issue of authority has direct bearing. On the job, at home, in church, and in government there are those who are set over us.

It is essential, then, that Christians learn how to properly respond to authority. For few things are more blameworthy before the eyes of the world than a Christian with a rebellious and haughty spirit.

But what about those times when authority is abused at your expense? Suffering under the blow of abusive authority carries a double-edged pain. It hurts because of the specific actions taking place. It also hurts because our trust in that authority has been betrayed.

What, then, do we do when authority is abused at our expense? How should you respond when your loyalty to those in authority is repaid with mistreatment? What happens when the suffering and pain you experience come from those who exercise authority over you? Are you still required to honor such authority? According to Peter, the answer is "Yes." Let's look and see what he means.

As **Group Leader,** *you* have a choice as to which elements best fit your group, your style of leadership, and your purposes. After you examine the **Session Objectives,** select the activities under each heading with which to begin your community building.

SESSION OBJECTIVES

√ Define how Christians are to relate to authority.
√ Analyze the connection between our submission to God and our relationship with those in authority.
√ Discuss how we are to respond to abusive authority.
√ Evaluate our response to specific situations in which authority is abused at our expense.

GETTING ACQUAINTED 20–25 minutes

Have a group member read aloud **Who's in Charge Here!** Then choose one or more of the following activities to help create a comfortable, nonthreatening atmosphere.

Sharing is for self-disclosure, not for seeking after right information. Allow your sharing to flow freely. Encourage group members to share without the fear that their comments will be considered trite.

Testing the Limits of Authority
Read through one statement at a time, and wait for each group member to circle his/her response before proceeding to the next statement. After you have finished, invite group members to share their responses, and any additional comments, to each statement in turn.

Ask: **As we think about the whole issue of authority, what single guiding principle would you suggest to someone in a position of authority, to help this person mold his/her relationships?**

Authority in Profile
Read one question at a time, state the options, and wait for each member to check an answer before proceeding to the

next question. Then invite group members to share their responses. Ask: **What do you think causes people to abuse their authority at the expense of others?**

GAINING INSIGHT 30–35 minutes

Peter and his readers were well acquainted with pain and suffering. They also knew firsthand what it felt like to be hurt by those who were in authority over them. The Christians to whom Peter wrote were being abused and persecuted by the Roman state—at the initiative of the king. Many were forced to flee for their lives. In spite of the situation, Peter gave his readers some very surprising counsel. He does not encourage them to resist. He especially does not condone subversive behavior. What he says can help shape our attitudes and perspectives when we face abusive authority. It may not make the hurting stop, but it might help us maintain our equilibrium.

Submitting Because God Said So

Before beginning, note that the kind of abuse Peter deals with has to do with mistreatment, false accusation, physical harm, and other such injustices. He is not dealing with the issue of a Christian being told to do something that is contrary to God's Word. That kind of abused authority is another issue, and the required response is much more clear-cut. The kind of abusive authority Peter is dealing with is much harder to handle. Read 1 Peter 2:13-17. Ask: **As you think about everything Peter says here, how can you summarize the foundational principle Peter is giving us?** (As we live in this world, Christians are to live within the confines of the authority structures that God Himself has established. The word "instituted" here refers to something that has been established by divine initiative and activity. The word "submit" means to voluntarily rank yourself under someone or something. Such voluntary submission is essential so that believers do not bring reproach on God's name through rebellious behavior.)

Ask: **Why was this important for those to whom Peter wrote?** (These Christians were being accused of inciting insurrection against the king. They were charged with crimes against the state. Therefore, he is challenging them to live voluntarily under the authority of the state to prove these accusations wrong.)

Point out to the group that this principle is important for us as well. While we may never be accused of crimes against the state, we may find ourselves falsely accused by those in authority. Others in authority may simply try to make us look bad for their own selfish gain. Even though this kind of abuse cuts deeply, we can outlive such accusations by a consistent lifestyle of goodness.

Ask: **How does exercising a submissive spirit help us show the world that we are "free men" and "servants of God"?** (When we voluntarily choose to exercise a submissive spirit, we are free to expend our energies in pursuing the well-being of others. We do not use our loyalties to Jesus Christ as an excuse for a rebellious and haughty spirit. Neither do we use our freedom in Christ as an excuse for indulging in a worldly lifestyle. As God's people, we are a positive force in the world rather than a negative influence. Our behavior becomes exemplary, and our lives say something very positive about God's personal rule within us.)

Ask: **Can a person who chooses not to exhibit a submissive spirit show proper respect for other people?** (Believers with a rebellious spirit are always at odds with others. They exhibit a need to gain an upper hand over other people. Their own best interests are always at stake. They are selfish people. But when a Christian chooses to live with a submissive spirit, it means that he or she has chosen to do what God expects. When we live under God's rule, we are able to treat others with the utmost respect. We are not compelled to compete with anyone, or jockey for position over anyone. We can hold everyone in proper esteem.)

In order to help your group understand the nature of God's order of authority, do the Scripture search activity. Focus their attention on the reasons these Scriptures give for recognizing this order of authority. Note the impact a believer's attitude toward authority has on his or her ability to have an effective witness in the world. Then do the response exercise, inviting group members to freely share how they feel about this foundational principle.

Submitting Apart From the Person

Comment: **In this passage, Peter shifts his focus from the larger issue of state authority to that of the household. Slavery was an integral part of life in the Roman Empire. Insurrection by slaves in a household was as serious as insurrection by citizens in the state. How slaves, particularly Christian slaves, related to their masters was just as important as how citizens related to the government. However, we need to keep in mind that what Peter is saying actually transcends the slave-master relationship. At a deeper level, Peter is presenting a nitty-gritty application of the same principle he discussed previously.** Read 1 Peter 2:18-19.

Ask: **How are slaves to relate to their masters?** (A slave can rebel against his master just as a citizen can rebel against the government. Slaves too have a choice to render voluntary obedience, in a spirit of submissiveness, not in a spirit of resentful compliance. They are to treat their masters with due respect and proper esteem. If by chance they serve a harsh master, the duty is still the same.)

Ask: **Why is it important for slaves to be submissive and respectful to even harsh masters?** (The character of the master is not the issue. The issue is the character of God and the Christian's relationship to Him. Whether the relationship is citizen-to-state, or slave-to-master, the Christian's obligation is to be conscious of the order of authority instituted by God. If a slave bears up under the pain of unjust treatment because he/she recognizes the work of God in his/her life, God's purposes will be fulfilled. This person will demonstrate the power of God, and God will be glorified as a result.)

Ask: **In order to show that you are being conscious of God, how can you relate to a person in authority who is harsh and abusive?** Let the group brainstorm to list ways to demonstrate the love of Christ to someone who abuses authority at their expense. After a list has been made, ask: **How will these things demonstrate the work of God in**

your life when you are responding to abusive authority? Direct the discussion to focus on issues such as good character, appropriate attitude, ethics of behavior, the "love your enemy" principle, etc. After a brief discussion, complete the exercise as directed in the book. Allow for open sharing. Ask for further explanation or clarification as appropriate.

Submitting When It Really Hurts
Comment: **It is always nice to know that someone has walked a difficult road before us. Such is the case in responding to those who abuse authority at our expense. Jesus is both our example and our encouragement.** Read 1 Peter 2:20-25.

Note that we can suffer for doing the wrong thing, and we can suffer for doing the right thing. If we suffer for doing the right thing, then we can learn from Jesus' response to undeserved punishment. Ask: **How was Jesus treated by those in authority?** (Jesus was unlawfully arrested and falsely accused. He suffered insults, beating, torture, and death.)

Ask: **Why was His treatment unjust?** (In verse 22 Peter quotes from Isaiah's prophecy about Jesus—Isaiah 53:9. He committed no sin. He committed no crime. He deceived no one by His life or teaching. Nevertheless, He was arrested and put to death. He deserved none of the treatment He received. He was punished by authorities who were motivated by selfishness, public image, and political standing.)

Ask: **How is Jesus our example in relating to those who abuse authority at our expense?** (We are called to suffer as Christ suffered; that is, to endure suffering for doing good. This is what God commends. Jesus made no attempt to retaliate or make threats against those who abused Him—although, as the Son of God, He certainly had both the power and opportunity. Rather, He patiently endured it all, and allowed God's work to be done. He understood that God Himself will bring the abusers into judgment in His own time. He, therefore, entrusted Himself to God, so that God's justice was free to work.)

Ask: **How will the Lord minister to us when we are unjustly abused?** (God has called us to a life of endurance, because He is the righteous judge. He will vindicate us in due time. Our souls have been committed to the One who gives diligent watch care over us. He guards and nurtures us. Through the suffering of Christ, we can have healing for our own suffering. Christ gives us strength to follow in His suffering, and respond as He responded.)

Invite group members to review their answers to this question and choose one thing that gives them the greatest encouragement when authority is abused at their expense. Make this time a group exercise in giving mutual support and encouragement. Encourage affirmation for those who are struggling with particularly abusive situations right now. As appropriate, draw parallels with Jesus' suffering.

GROWING BY DOING 20–25 minutes

Fashion a Response

Lead the group through the exercise in their books. Then divide them into discussion teams of three to four to share their answers. After each person shares, the others in the team can offer additional suggestions for consideration (not more than two suggestions for each principle). Each discussion team should close in prayer.

A Case in Point

Instruct group members to complete the exercise in their books. Then invite volunteers to share their case studies. Allow the group to suggest ways the principles from this study might apply to each case presented. After you are done, ask: **Are there ever situations Christians encounter in which you think they *should not* submit to abusive authority? If so, describe such a situation.**

Pointing Out Specifics

In teams of three to four, encourage group members to openly discuss their struggles in relation to the principles of this study. After completing the exercise, group members should share one prayer request relating to this exercise. Close with a time of supportive prayer.

GOING THE SECOND MILE 5 minutes

Challenge the group to spend some time during the next week seeking the spirit of Jesus in how they respond to abusive authority. The personal prayer exercise can help them grow in the example of Jesus.

GROWING AS A LEADER

How well do you know the members of your small group? A very significant role a small group leader can play is that of a shepherd, and a facilitator of mutual care. Group leaders are often in a position of having access to information about the hurts, joys, and burdens of their small group members. Small group members will often confide in their leaders. They will seek them out for counsel and advice. Consequently, small group leaders can put group members in touch with each other for mutual support and encouragement. After all, this is part of what a small group is for—to provide a supportive network of relationships.

As a small group leader, you can enhance this process by taking the initiative to know your group members. The more they feel you are their friend, the more you can encourage the process of group caring and ministry to one another. Try a few of these suggestions.

- ❑ Spend time socializing with your group members. Do things with them outside of group time. Shared meals, game nights, or just visiting together can open deeper levels of relationships with your group members. These social times can happen with one family at a time, or with several people from the group. Male leaders can go out to breakfast with the men of the group. Female leaders can gather the women together for coffee.
- ❑ Contact each group member once a month. This quick check-up contact to see how things are going can go a long way in building supportive relationships.
- ❑ Be sensitive to recognize group members on special days or for special achievements. It is just as important to do

this personally, as it is to do it in the group context.

- ❑ Be there in difficult times. Always be available to assist group members going through tough times. Anyone can send a card or make a prayer request. It takes a concerned friend to be involved.

FIVE

Enduring What You Don't Deserve

No matter how spiritually mature we are, we are going to suffer difficult things. Circumstances are going to work against us at times. People will abuse us. But most especially, we will have to endure unjust and painful treatment we do not deserve.

It is important, then, for Christians to understand what God expects during those times when life knocks us around. For, God has not called us to understand the mysteries of life, or to engage in philosophical debate about suffering. He calls us to respond to suffering in a way that is worthy of the name of Christ.

Peter's concern in this passage is to help us develop the kind of perspective that will help us respond during those times when we suffer for doing good.

As **Group Leader,** *you* have a choice as to which elements best fit your group, your style of leadership, and your purposes. After you examine the **Session Objectives**, select the activities under each heading with which to begin your community building.

SESSION OBJECTIVES

- √ Discuss how a Christian should respond when suffering for doing good.
- √ Define the kind of response to unjust treatment that will give the best witness for our faith.
- √ Recall the sufferings of Christ and receive encouragement from His example.

GETTING ACQUAINTED 15–20 minutes

Have a group member read aloud **I Get No Respect!** Then choose one or more of the following activities to help create a comfortable, nonthreatening atmosphere.

Animal Instincts

Read through one statement at a time, and wait for each group member to circle their response before proceeding to the next statement. After you have finished, invite group members to share their responses to each statement in turn. Ask for explanations as responses are shared.

GAINING INSIGHT 35–40 minutes

The walls can squeeze us pretty tight when we suffer in spite of doing that which is right and good. How can we respond to such pressure? Often we think if we could only strike back we would sure feel a lot better. However, that is not a distinctively Christian response, is it? Let's look at the counsel Peter offers for handling the hurt of suffering for doing good.

Live in Harmony

Read 1 Peter 3:8. Ask: **What picture does the word *harmony* conjure up in your mind?** Lead your group through the creative expression activity. Encourage them to be as creative as they desire. For those having difficulty getting started, offer some examples such as: a symphony orchestra, a bicycle wheel, an ant colony or beehive. Invite group members to share and explain their drawings.

Note that the word *harmony* is unique when applied to relationships between Christians. It refers to cooperation, working together, persevering with one another, and unity. It is the opposite of autonomy, individualism, competition, selfish ambition, or self-serving motivation.

Ask: **Why would Peter give this advice to Christians who were suffering from harsh abuse and unjust treatment?** (Peter probably knew that even Christians can get cranky and difficult when they are under pressure. It is easy to project onto someone else the anger you feel because of your pain. It is easy to turn inward and become aloof, holding others at arm's length, and not letting them support you through your pain. Trust can become a problem. Even Christians can hurt so badly they shut everyone else out. Hence, Peter's words are a reminder of the need to maintain those essential faith relationships that can bring the kind of support we need into the midst of our hurt.)

Ask: **What qualities does Peter say should be present in order for Christians to live in harmony with each other?** Help the group define the various qualities Peter gives. Use the following information as appropriate:

Sympathy—to share the joys and sorrows of life with one another; to weep with those who weep and rejoice with those who rejoice.

Love as brothers—the kind of love you would expect to find in a family; the enjoyment of being together in a common bond.

Compassion—not only to feel something with another person, but to be moved to do something about it; acting decisively out of concern for someone else.

Humility—acting in preference toward others, without any hint of self-assertiveness, or thought of personal gain or ambition; genuinely appreciating the worth of others without any need to be recognized in return.

Ask: **How do these various qualities help build and maintain harmony between believers?** (When Christians are consciously looking out for the interests and welfare of each other, rather than looking out for their own best interests, they develop a nurturing supportive fellowship. This is the kind of fellowship where people's hurts can be healed, and difficulties eased. We move beyond simply tolerating each other's weaknesses to affirming the good God has for each of us.)

Minister God's Blessing

Read 1 Peter 3:9-12. Comment: **Peter makes it clear that if we know Jesus Christ, then we have been called to the ministry of blessing others. It is not our option to call down curses on those who cause our pain. But we are to show an active kindness to them and willingly extend God's blessing.**

Ask: **Is this easy or difficult for you to do? Why?** Invite group members to voluntarily share their answers to this question. Be sure each one is allowed to share without feeling the threat of negative value judgments.

Ask: **What promises does Peter give for those who minister God's blessing to others?** Lead the group to list the various things Peter states. Indicate that when we make peace in the midst of suffering, we prove we are God's children. His blessing will naturally fall on our lives, and He will be attentive to our needs. We can count on His loving concern. This does not mean the pain will go away. It does mean that, in the midst of suffering for doing good, God will bring a greater awareness of His presence into our experience.

Ask: **Looking over all that Peter says here, what is most likely to motivate you to minister God's blessing to those who abuse you? What least motivates you?** Entertain responses, once again being sure to avoid any negative value judgments on what someone shares. Then lead the group to list a number of specific actions they can take to minister God's blessing to those who unjustly hurt them.

Ask: **How well do you do when you measure yourself next to this list?** Have the group complete the self-evaluation activity as directed in their books. Invite sharing, asking for explanation or clarification as appropriate.

Be a Ready Witness

Read 1 Peter 3:13-16. Ask: **What specifically are we to be ready to share with those who ask?** (Peter tells us to be ready to share the reason for our hope in Jesus Christ. But sharing the reason for our hope is much more than telling someone why we are a Christian, or how we became one. To share the reason for our hope in the midst of our hurt refers to our whole life perspective. It refers to how we view that which happens to us in this life, because of what we anticipate when our hope comes to completion.)

Ask: **Why will this quality of hope be evident to others when we suffer for doing good?** (When we patiently endure suffering, with an attitude of hopeful anticipation of our eternal reward, we will stand in stark contrast to the rest of the world. Living with a sense of hope in the midst of pain is not the norm. Our perspective and attitude removes the need to retaliate or create our own defense. We can rest in our relationship with Jesus, and radiate His hope at a time when others would be hopeless.)

Ask: **How are we to share our hope with those who ask? Why is this significant?** (Peter indicates that we should speak with gentleness and respect toward those who ask. In other words, the manner of our speech should reflect the nature of our hope—it should be positive, joyful, and attractive. Responding in harshness is contrary to the meaning of our hope. A haughty or condescending spirit will only make us blameworthy and make our message undesirable. We should also be able to speak with a clear conscience, so those who unjustly abuse us will be put to shame for what they do.)

Work through the "grade card" activity in the book. Divide into smaller teams to discuss responses. Direct teams to discuss ways to improve their ready witness grade.

Receive the Blessing of Jesus

Read 1 Peter 3:17-18, 21b-22. Ask: **As you read and reflect on Peter's words, how would you describe the blessing**

that came to Jesus? (Jesus also suffered for doing good. He experienced the ultimate pain and sacrifice as a result. Yet, by enduring, Jesus brought us back to God. We can receive forgiveness for our sin. And through His resurrection from the dead, He is now exalted by God above all powers and authorities, spiritual and human. Those who unjustly abused Him are now under His sovereign rule. For enduring the ultimate suffering, He has received the ultimate blessing.)

Ask: **How does that blessing enter our experiences when we suffer for doing good?** (Through salvation in Jesus, we can rest in God's care. Jesus knows our hurt, because He too was wounded. Because Jesus is now exalted, He exercises His authority on our behalf—leading, guiding, directing, and protecting. Seated at the right hand of God, He intercedes for us before the Father, releasing the fullness of His love and grace into our pain. Ultimately, we too will be exalted with Christ above our abusers.)

Encourage the group to complete the "word picture" activity in their books. Share and discuss what they have written. Focus discussion on how Jesus' blessing can be a positive force to continue doing good; particularly when we are suffering unjustly.

GROWING BY DOING 20–25 minutes

Learning by Example
Together, read the Scripture passages about each character, and list ways each one demonstrated the principles of this study in response to unjust suffering. Also note how God blessed them as a result. Then divide into smaller discussion teams to share how you can each demonstrate these same qualities when you suffer for doing good.

Making It Personal
Complete the activity in the book. Then divide into smaller discussion teams to share responses. Each team should spend the balance of their time praying for each other.

GOING THE SECOND MILE 5 minutes

Note that God's Word contains a great deal of comfort for us when we suffer for doing good. Encourage your group to make this comfort their own by completing this section on their own this week.

GROWING AS A LEADER

In any learning setting it is possible that someone will give an answer to a question that is not the "right" answer. Occasionally, people will give answers that are a little "off the wall." How you handle these situations may well determine the openness of your group. While it is important to be faithful to the meaning of God's Word, it is also important that group members feel affirmed for their contribution and participation. But how do you achieve this kind of environment when people give wrong answers?

First, using both verbal and nonverbal cues, always make it clear that every contribution is welcomed and accepted. It is not necessary to make negative value judgments on a given answer. A wrong answer need not sidetrack your discussion. Rather, use every answer as a springboard toward greater understanding of how God's Word applies to life.

Second, create an atmosphere that says, "We are in a process of discovery together." Allow discussion to continue in spite of any wrong answer you may receive. Encouraging a thinking-out-loud type of discussion format will take the pressure off you and other group members, to respond to answers that are not quite appropriate.

Third, avoid using a lot of black-and-white type questions, or rhetorical questions where the answer is already a given. Use questions that encourage exploration of the biblical text. Focus on questions that encourage personal reflection and application.

Last, always keep in mind that you are all at different stages of spiritual development. You do not all possess the same clarity of thought in Bible study, or in discerning spiritual issues. Nurture the mentality that your small group is a hothouse for spiritual growth and development.

SIX

Waiting for It All to End

The Christian life can be accurately described as a period of waiting. As Christians, we live between the now and the not yet; the period of time when the kingdom of God has been established, but has not yet reached its final consummation. We live between the new birth and the return of our Lord in glory.

So, what should we do while we are waiting for it all to end? This is an especially appropriate question when that period of waiting involves painful trials. Peter gives several important pieces of advice to help us make the best of our time while we wait for it all to end.

As **Group Leader,** *you* have a choice as to which elements best fit your group, your style of leadership, and your purposes. After you examine the **Session Objectives,** select the activities under each heading with which to begin your community building.

SESSION OBJECTIVES

√ Delineate specific ways to be involved in ministry to others while waiting for our Lord to return.
√ Discuss the need to be involved in ministry during this period of waiting for our Lord to return.
√ Define ways to be effective through the ministries Peter describes.
√ Establish a personal action plan for doing ministry during this period of waiting for our Lord to return.

GETTING ACQUAINTED 15–20 minutes

Have a group member read aloud **Watching Time Go By.** Then choose one of the following activities to help create a more comfortable, nonthreatening atmosphere.

Pocket Principle

1 The whole group question-and-answer approach to discussion and personal sharing may not create the kind of communication patterns that encourage good group bonding. More assertive members will tend to dominate at the expense of quieter ones. Make use of discussion techniques that will involve the greatest number of people at any given time.

Memorable Moments
Direct group members to complete the first part of the exercise individually. When group members are finished, read each statement and invite response. Note any similarities, or ask for further explanation as appropriate. Then divide into smaller teams of three to four to discuss the second part of the activity. After ample time for discussion, call the group back together and ask: **Generally speaking, is waiting a problem for you? Why or why not?**

While You Wait
Lead the group through the exercise in their books. Then divide into smaller teams to share their answers. After ade-

quate discussion time, call the group back together and ask: **In your mind, what would be the ideal waiting posture to assume during your waiting experiences?**

GAINING INSIGHT 35–40 minutes

Usually the word *passive* is an accurate term to describe how we spend our time waiting. However, Peter's words have much more to do with being active rather than passive. In fact, if we do what Peter says, we will have more than enough to do while we are waiting for it all to end. Peter calls us to engage in three very active ministries during this period of waiting.

The Ministry of Prayer

Read 1 Peter 4:7. Ask: **Is it easy or difficult for you to maintain an effective ministry of prayer during painful times?** Allow for a brief period of open sharing. Encourage group members to share their personal struggles with prayer in the midst of hurtful circumstances. Ask for personal illustrations where appropriate. Help the group members feel okay about themselves when they have difficulty praying during tough times. Help them understand that this is common. However, we do need at least to understand why Peter feels that this ministry of prayer is so important.

Ask: **Why do you think Peter believes this is such an important ministry while we are waiting for Jesus to return?** (Because Jesus' return is imminent, believers should live their lives with a heightened sense of spiritual values. We should live our lives in the shadow of eternity. The best way to live with the awareness of eternity is to exercise the ministry of prayer. Through the ministry of prayer we can learn to take the right things seriously. God's will can be revealed to us. His values can become part of our thinking. His power can have an open channel to flow freely in the midst of our hurt.)

Ask: **How are a clear mind and self-control related to an effective ministry of prayer?** (By exercising self-control we can keep our mind clear about what really matters in our lives. Keeping a clear mind in relation to spiritual values keeps us from having a strictly horizontal perspective [i.e., seeing everything in terms of the physical and earthly, rather than the spiritual]. All of this impacts our ability to seek after God's mind in prayer.)

Comment: **Peter, of all people, knew what it meant to practice the ministry of prayer. He himself had failed in this very thing. When Jesus asked Peter to keep watch in prayer with Him in the Garden of Gethsemane, Peter kept falling asleep. Peter learned about the importance of prayer from his own failure. But he also learned from the example of Jesus. We can too.**

Use the Scripture analysis activity to help group members learn from Jesus how they can have an effective ministry of prayer during the painful times of life.

The Ministry of Forbearance

Ask: **What does the word *forbearance* mean?** Entertain a few responses. Indicate that the word simply defines a relationship marked by mutual tolerance. Read 1 Peter 4:8-9.

Note the background of the word *deeply* in verse 8. Ask: **How does this word picture help you better understand Peter's charge about loving other believers?** (For a horse to run full-tilt involves extreme strain. Every muscle is applied to the task. Loving each other deeply can involve this kind of stress and strain. It means working hard to overlook *all* that we do not like in other people. Other people's faults will always challenge our acceptance of them. In working to love each other deeply, we can extend to each other the grace o God, just as it has been extended to us.)

Ask: **What is hospitality and how does offering hospitality without grumbling or complaining relate to the practice of mutual toleration?** (Hospitality is the practical act o courtesy and graciousness in providing for the needs of others. However, this can be more difficult than it sounds. We can get under each other's skin. People act differently than we expect. Many times we feel that it's all we can do to meet our own needs, let alone the needs of others. Hospital ity is often inconvenient and can easily result in disappointed expectations. But, in essence, it is an effort to show others that we love them deeply through offering hospitality without grumbling or complaining about the inconvenience.)

Explain to the group how important hospitality was in the early church. Churches did not have meeting places. They met in each other's homes. Also, in a time of persecution, when Christians were on the move, simple lodging was a necessity. Hosting guests in either case could be a huge inconvenience. It was possible for personalities to clash in such close quarters. The unspoken expectations for how a guest should act could be violated. Adequate provisions could be a problem. Hence, Peter challenges his readers with a practical application of the "love others deeply" principle. They should not begrudge each other this simple courtesy. They should extend it without grumbling or complaining about the inconvenience, because of the love they share in Jesus Christ. And we too should do the same.

Divide into smaller work teams to complete the evaluation activity. Each team should design their own evaluation tool as directed in their books. Each member should then share with his/her team at least one way to improve in the ministry of forbearance.

Allow individual group members the opportunity to practice using their spiritual gifts within the group. Let your group be a hothouse for ministry to one another through the spiritual gifts of group members.

The Ministry of Service

Read 1 Peter 4:10-11. Ask: **How does Peter direct us to use our spiritual gifts in service?** (Actually, Peter says two things. First, through the Holy Spirit, God has given us these gifts as a trust. The phrase "faithfully administering" (verse 10) refers to stewardship. That is, we do not own these gifts; we are simply acting as managers on God's behalf. Therefore, we should each be faithful in this trust, using our gifts ungrudgingly for the good of others. Second, we should use our gifts with the awareness that God Himself is empowering us to do so. It is through His strength and by His word that we are able to use our gifts in service to others.)

Ask: **What is the goal of using our gifts?** (Since it is God who empowers us to use these gifts, it is God who will be praised as a result. Our focus in using our spiritual gifts should always be to bring glory, honor, and praise to God. To do otherwise reduces our service to selfishness and pride, and elevates the gift above the Giver. To administer our gifts faithfully, we must always keep in mind that God's glory is in it. That God is glorified through our ministry of service is our crowning satisfaction.)

Comment: **We are each unique, and this means that each one of us has a unique calling in the ministry of service. One of the important factors in discerning and using our spiritual gifts is the confirmation of other believers. Sometimes others can see things in us that we cannot see ourselves.**

Lead the group through the spiritual gifts inventory activity in their books. Structure this activity to be a real time of mutual affirmation for your group members.

To help your group understand the importance of glorifying God through our ministry of service, divide into smaller teams to complete the first part of the evaluation exercise as directed in the book. Call the group back together and complete the second part of the exercise. As group members share, invite further comments and explanation as appropriate.

GROWING BY DOING 20–25 minutes

Marking Time
Lead the group through the exercise in their books. Then divide into smaller discussion teams for sharing. Instruct each team to conclude their sharing with a time of supportive prayer.

GOING THE SECOND MILE 5 minutes

Encourage your group to begin their process of ministry by expressing appreciation for those who have ministered to them. They can do so by completing this section on their own during the next week.

GROWING AS A LEADER

What kind of communication pattern is your group developing? All small groups develop a certain pattern of communication. For some groups, this pattern is established very early in group life. For other groups, the pattern takes some time to evolve. In either case, there are three types of communication patterns that can be identified.

The first pattern is when communication happens primarily between the leader and individuals in the group, but not between group members. This is a one-way pattern, with the group leader as the focal point. All communication begins with the leader and returns to the leader.

The second pattern is when communication takes place between the leader and dominant group members, and between dominant group members themselves. The basic difference between this pattern and the previous is that here certain individuals do communicate directly with each other. However, it does not involve the entire group. The strongest personalities carry the discussion as directed by the leader.

The third pattern is that of total group communication. It occurs when the leader is seen as part of the group, rather than as someone who directs the discussion of individuals. Group members are free to engage each other without first going through the leader. All members are participants, not just the dominant personalities.

A number of factors can impact the pattern your group establishes: your leadership style, individual personalities, the format of your meeting, the types of questions you ask, the expectations of group members regarding their own participation. Be attentive to the pattern of communication your group is developing, and strive to involve all group members in the process of communication.

SEVEN

Going from Bad to Worse

Have you ever noticed how much time we spend reacting to problems or crises in our lives? Consequently, we lose a great deal of joy. Our attitude becomes dull—even sour. At times, it seems like things just do not get any better—that things have gone from bad to worse.

This is especially true when we begin suffering because we are Christians. Life is tough enough without the threat of suffering for what we believe. After all, a personal faith is just that—it is personal. Why should our faith in Christ bother anyone else, right? Wouldn't it be nice if life were that simple?

However, such suffering need not sap our joy. We can still be joyful when we are under attack for being Christians. Peter thought so, at least. He and his people were suffering for no other reason than the fact they were Christians. But throughout this passage, Peter's attitude is joyful. Let's see what his secret is.

As **Group Leader,** *you* have a choice as to which elements best fit your group, your style of leadership, and your purposes. After you examine the **Session Objectives**, select the activities under each heading with which to begin your community building.

SESSION OBJECTIVES

√ Discuss the problem of suffering because of our faith in Jesus Christ.
√ Analyze our attitude during those periods when our faith is under fire by non-Christians.
√ Express trust in God for the strength to do His will when we suffer for being Christians.

GETTING ACQUAINTED 20–25 minutes

Have a group member read aloud **Turning up the Heat.** Then choose one or more of the following activities to help create a comfortable, nonthreatening atmosphere.

A Closer Look
Read through one statement at a time, and wait for each group member to write their response before proceeding to the next statement. After you have finished, invite group members to share their responses to each statement in turn. Ask for explanations or further comments as appropriate. Ask: **Considering where you are right now in your life, what would be the most difficult persecution for you to face?**

GAINING INSIGHT 30–35 minutes

Pocket Principle

1 Listen carefully during discussion times so you can summarize the primary ideas brought up in discussion before continuing to the next question. This will help bring closure to the groups' thoughts. It will also provide smoother transition from one question to the next.

From What Perspective Do You View Painful Trials?
Read 1 Peter 4:12-13. Ask: **According to what Peter says, what are the two perspectives from which we can view suffering for Jesus' name?** (People with the first per-

spective see suffering as strange and abnormal. They are bewildered and dismayed when they have to endure pain because they are Christians. People with the second perspective see suffering for Jesus as part of the natural course of life. In fact, they expect to suffer painful trials for their faith because Jesus likewise suffered. They know that by enduring sufferings, they are participating in Jesus' sufferings.)

Ask: **How does our perspective affect the conclusions we draw about our difficult experiences?** (The way we approach a problem will naturally determine the way we reach our conclusion—and, sometimes, the conclusion we reach. If, as Christians, we expect ease and comfort, we will draw negative conclusions when we experience any level of pain. Eventually, drawing negative conclusions about painful experiences can lead to cynicism and fatalism. However, if we expect to suffer as Jesus suffered, we can rejoice at our privilege to share in His suffering.)

Ask: **Why does Peter consider it a privilege to participate in the sufferings of Christ?** (We live in a world hostile to the claims and cause of Jesus. If the world persecuted Him, why should we expect any less? Hence, when we suffer as Christ suffered, we prove we are His. Our suffering can help us see the urgency and importance of the work He began on earth, and our part in it.)

Ask: **How can this perspective produce a joyful attitude in suffering?** (By taking the way of the cross, Jesus suffered immense pain. Yet, in the end, He was glorified and honored. If we suffer as He suffered, we likewise will share in His glory and victory when He returns. This is cause for joy now.)

For What Reasons Do You Suffer?

Read 1 Peter 4:14-16. Ask: **What are the right and wrong reasons for suffering, as Peter gives them?** Work together to fill in the chart with the information Peter gives. Note for the group how Peter lists meddling along with being a criminal. Use this to help the group understand the many ways to suffer for the wrong reason. While few of us will ever suffer as a thief or murderer, we may create other problems for ourselves. Ask: **What other ways of suffering for the wrong reason can we list that would be on the same level as "meddler"?**

Ask: **Why do you suppose Peter feels the necessity to warn these Christians about suffering for the wrong reasons?** (Suffering for the wrong reasons brings far greater shame than suffering for the right reasons. When believers suffer for the wrong reasons, they call their Christian testimony into question. They cause the world to look suspiciously at the church. The claims of the Gospel become suspect. Hence, believers need to always be evaluating themselves to be sure they are suffering for the cause of Christ. For, when our faith is under fire, it can be easy to take the path of least resistance and try to fit into the world around us.)

Ask: **Why is suffering for the sake of Christ a blessing?** (Suffering for Jesus' name demonstrates that God is at work in our lives. It says His grace is active. It confirms the promise that His Spirit will rest on us, and that His glory will be revealed in our lives.)

Ask: **How should this shape your attitude toward the painful times when your faith is under fire?** (There is nothing to be ashamed of when we suffer for being a Christian. Rather, we can rejoice that God is at work in our lives through His Spirit. We can rejoice that His glory will be revealed through our suffering. Therefore, we can live a life of praise to God because we bear the name of Christ.)

What Is Your Future Prospect?

Read 1 Peter 4:17-18. Ask: **How would you describe the difference between the judgment Christians face and that of the unbeliever?** After some discussion ask: **How does the present judgment believers experience prepare us for the future glory we will receive when Jesus returns?** (First, there is a judgment that comes to the house of God. This is a present judgment that prepares us for our future glory. The painful trials and sufferings we experience at the hands of others, God uses as a means to prove our faithfulness. It cleanses us from our impurities and draws us closer to Him. It establishes our dedication. Through it, we can demonstrate our loyalty to Jesus when our faith is under fire. Second, there is the judgment of the unbeliever. It is a final judgment that will come to those who have chosen to reject the Gospel of Christ and live disobediently to God.)

Help your group understand the full intent of Peter's words. His comparison of the believer's judgment, over against that of the unbeliever, is meant to be a comfort. If we think our life on earth is difficult because of our faith in Jesus, or that our trials are intense, then think how much worse the judgment of the unbeliever will be. For, if leading a righteous life opens us to opposition and abuse, how much worse will judgment be for the unbeliever who has rejected God.

Ask: **How can this perspective of judgment bring joy into your life when you suffer for Jesus' name?** (When we realize that God's purpose in allowing these painful trials is to prepare us for His glory, we have a reason to be joyful. While the pain will not necessarily be any less, it can be tolerable because of what we know is waiting at the other end. We should, then, graciously receive all of God's working in our lives when our faith is under fire. Because we know what God's intentions are, we can find true joy in releasing ourselves to His preparatory work.)

How Is Your Commitment When Your Faith Is Under Fire?

Read 1 Peter 4:19. Ask: **What do you think Peter means by the phrase "suffer according to God's will"?** (Peter is telling us that nothing is allowed to enter our lives without God's consent. All that happens to us happens with His knowledge, and for His purposes. Even the difficult times of suffering and pain can be used by God to work out His good purposes in our lives. Hence, the pain we experience is only that which is within the parameters of His will for us. Whatever we suffer God will use to fulfill His plan and purposes; to further His will and promote His glory in our lives.)

Ask: **What kind of commitment is Peter calling us to exercise?** (Peter speaks of a two-part commitment. The first part is to have full trust in the keeping power of God. The word Peter uses for *commit* is a financial term. In Peter's day they did not have banks. A person leaving home on a long journey would place his money in the safe keeping of one he could trust. That trust was sacred. To break it was a great offense. This is the kind of commitment Peter is challenging us to make; a commitment to place ourselves completely in God's hands.

The second part of this commitment is to live our lives in a manner that reflects our trust in God. Committing ourselves into God's care involves getting on with the business of living a life of good deeds. As believers, we are not called to be known by what we suffer, but by how we live and what we do. We cannot actively commit ourselves to God's keeping and do good if we have fixated on our own suffering. Peter is essentially saying that we are to commit ourselves to God, then get on with what Christians are called to do.)

Ask: **What can we count on when we make that kind of commitment to God?** (Peter calls God the "faithful Creator." All power is His. When we suffer for being Christians, we can place ourselves in the hands of God with the full assurance that He will guard our deposit with complete faithfulness. In that trust we can find joy in the midst of our suffering.)

GROWING BY DOING 20–25 minutes

Pocket Principle

2 When asking your group to share something personal, allow them the privilege of not feeling rushed or hurried. Often, it takes people a little time to collect their thoughts, and to prepare themselves for self-disclosure.

Choosing Your Joy

Lead the group through the exercise in their books. Then divide into smaller discussion teams of three to four to share responses. Group members should indicate how the statement they chose can strengthen them when their faith is under fire.

After ample time for discussion, call the group back together and form a prayer circle. Ask group members to give a brief prayer expressing trust based on what they just shared.

Optional—Jesus Said It Would Happen
As a large group, read through the Scripture passages as directed in the book. Then discuss the accompanying questions.

GOING THE SECOND MILE 5 minutes

Remind group members to complete this section on their own during the next week.

GROWING AS A LEADER

The appearance of the classroom is often taken for granted. But the fact is, physical environment can have as big an impact on how your group interacts as any relational factor. Learning environment is a subtle, yet powerful, aspect of effective group life. As you prepare your session material, think about how the physical environment will impact the group's interaction. The following checklist will help you take stock of your meeting arrangements.

- ❑ Is the room well lighted?
- ❑ Does the room have proper ventilation?
- ❑ Is your room neat and clean? Is it attractive and inviting?
- ❑ Is the size of the room appropriate for the size of your group?
- ❑ Does the chair arrangement allow face-to-face contact?
- ❑ Does the furniture group members sit in encourage discussion, or is it uncomfortable? Is it too comfortable?
- ❑ Is the room temperature set at a comfortable level?
- ❑ Does the room size/arrangement allow you to use smaller groupings if desired? Does the furniture allow it?
- ❑ Can you comfortably use additional teaching equipment, such as a chalkboard, wall charts, screens, overhead projector, etc.?
- ❑ Does the room size allow your group to grow?
- ❑ Is there a good place to set up refreshments if desired?

EIGHT

Called to Glory

YOU are called to glory! There is no greater promise for Christians than that. God Himself has called all who believe in Jesus Christ to enter into eternal glory with Him. He paid for it. He promised it. And He fully intends to deliver!

What more can God say to people who are hurting and suffering in a difficult and hostile world? What other handle do we need to take hold of when the walls of pain start closing in on us? For, when God calls us, He commits Himself to us. If He has committed Himself to bringing us into this eternal glory, then that is just where He will take us.

But what about the pain along the way? In Peter's closing words he gives four final encouragements to help us maneuver through any painful difficulty we encounter on our road to glory.

As **Group Leader,** *you* have a choice as to which elements best fit your group, your style of leadership, and your purposes. After you examine the **Session Objectives,** select the activities under each heading with which to begin your community building.

SESSION OBJECTIVES

√ Delineate and discuss the various helps we have to assist us in our journey to eternal glory with Jesus.
√ Share personal stories of each one's individual journey on the road to eternal glory.
√ Express gratitude to God for His care in our lives during the painful times of our journey to eternal glory.

GETTING ACQUAINTED 15–20 minutes

Have a group member read aloud **Remember the Goal.** Then choose one or more of the following activities to help create a comfortable, nonthreatening atmosphere.

Pocket Principle

1 **As you lead, be sensitive to why your members are there. Work to assist them in expressing their needs and their agendas for being at the group meeting.**

My Life Story

Instruct group members to complete the activity individually. After about five to eight minutes, invite members to share responses. Ask for additional comments and explanation. Note any similarities in what is shared. Discuss:

- ❑ **Which of these books sounds the most interesting to you? Why?**
- ❑ **If your book came to print, who do you think would benefit most from reading it?**
- ❑ **How would you evaluate the contents of these various books? Do they sound the same, or are they significantly different?**

Famous Last Words

Complete the exercise as directed in the book. Then discuss:

- ❑ **Why are these the most important words for you to leave?**
- ❑ **In what way do these words reflect your "guiding principles" in life?**

❑ **What do your last words say about the importance of God in your life?**

Let's Take a Trip

Read through one statement at a time, state the options, and give group members time to check an answer before proceeding to the next statement. After you have finished, invite group members to share their responses.

GAINING INSIGHT 35–40 minutes

Pocket Principle

2 Keep Bible study a central part of your small group meeting. God's Word gives us a picture of the world as it really is, and as God sees it. Through it we define who we are as God's people.

The Stepping Stone of Humility

Read 1 Peter 5:5b-6. Ask: **What does Peter mean to "clothe yourselves with humility"?** Divide into smaller groups to do the "dictionary definition" exercise. Call the group together after ample time and ask for responses. Help the group understand that Peter is dealing with an overall attitude and perspective from which we view other people—both Christian and non-Christian. True humility is much harder to define than to recognize. It is not a feeling of worthlessness or weakness, an eagerness to please others, or lack of self-confidence. It is an attitude of genuine interest in pursuing the well-being of others, while maintaining a realistic appraisal of your own self-worth. Humility helps us see others as being of great worth to God, and helps us respond accordingly in willing service.

Ask: **How does humility influence our relationships with other believers?** (Humility will determine the quality of our relationships within the Christian community. Our ability to get along will be directly proportionate to the depth of our humility. Lack of genuine humility eventually produces self-serving relationships, and a deterioration of spiritual fellowship. When we exercise genuine humility, we desire to help others be all that God intended them to be.)

Ask: **How does humility assist us through the painful times?** (It is much easier to accept what God has for us in the painful times when we exhibit a spirit of humility. Lack of humility, through a proud or haughty spirit, results in fighting against our pain or the perceived causes. In such cases, God's purposes are of little concern. However, when we are humble we are freed to open ourselves to God's work through our experiences. Our only concern is to allow God's process to come to completion in our lives through our pain.)

Ask: **How is humility before God related to humility toward others?** (True humility begins when we learn to bow before God, recognizing our place in His plan, and seeing ourselves through His eyes.)

Ask: **How will God honor those who are truly humble before Him?** (Peter's reference to God's mighty hand indicates that He is in complete and sovereign control of our lives and circumstances. By submitting to that control, His purposes can be fulfilled at the time He decides is best.)

Lead the group through the "humility quotient" exercise in their books. Help the group to recognize that real humility does not come easily for most people. It takes work to be humble before God and each other, but it is not impossible. Allowing God His rightful place of control in our lives is the beginning point. Under His hand we can receive the grace we need to exhibit humility in our relationships.

The Stepping Stone of Dependence

Read 1 Peter 5:7. Ask: **How does casting our anxiety on God demonstrate our dependence on Him?** (Note that Peter refers to our anxieties, and not the problem itself. It is easy to give our problems to God and still be anxious about them. But Peter tells us that it is when we give our anxieties to God we can really begin to trust in God's care. Giving our anxieties to God indicates that we really do believe He is able to handle things. We can leave the worry, so to speak, up to God. We can be released from our preoccupation with our problem, and recognize and experience God's care.)

Ask: **For what do you most need to depend on God dur-**

ing painful times? Encourage open sharing. Affirm all responses that are given.

Comment: **Peter seems to be implying that God cannot demonstrate His care in our lives if we do not cast our anxieties on Him. What do you think about that?** Once again, allow for open sharing. Help the group understand that God is always able to demonstrate His care. However, if we hold onto our worries and concerns about a particular problem, we may not always be able to recognize God's care.

Lead the group through the reflection and checklist exercises, as directed in their books. Then divide into smaller groups for sharing.

The Stepping Stone of Resistance
Read 1 Peter 5:8-9. Ask: **What can we learn about the devil in these verses?** (The word Peter uses for *enemy* is a legal term referring to an opponent in a lawsuit that is out to soak you for all you are worth. The term *devil* means "one who slanders and deceives." The devil is a powerful, vicious, and cunning adversary who preys on those who are unaware. He is constantly in search of someone to destroy through any means possible. For him, there is no such thing as compromise, truce, or cease-fire. He is relentless in his pursuit to work spiritual destruction.)

Ask: **How are we most vulnerable to the devil during painful times?** (Our defenses are at their lowest point when we are in the midst of pain and hurt. We do not always think clearly when under great stress. Sometimes we can be angry, or otherwise emotionally stretched by our hurt. At such times, we may not be able to recognize the devil's temptations for what they are. We may not be as discerning as we should be. All of this makes us quite vulnerable.)

Ask: **How can we respond to the devil?** (Peter instructs us in three ways. First, we need to maintain self-control, and be ever aware. In other words, we need to maintain mental composure and sound mind so we can recognize our enemy for who and what he is. Second, we are to stand firm and resist him. We should take the posture of leaning forward in battle, actively resisting the devil in the strength of our faith. If we run, he will run after us. If we resist, he will fail and flee. Third, we are to take courage from the fellowship of believers. We are not alone in this battle. Many fellow believers fight alongside us. From their partnership and example, we can gain strength and encouragement.)

Ask: **Noting what Peter says in verse 9, how would you characterize the relationship between the devil and suffering?** (While it would be inaccurate to say that all suffering is caused by the devil, it is appropriate to say that the devil is capable of causing people to suffer. Mostly, the devil's tactic is to work through a human agent to cause wreckage and ruin in people's lives. How much suffering the devil inflicts directly is something we will probably never know.)

Use the Scripture search activity to help your group understand more about how the devil can impact us when we are in difficult times.

The Stepping Stone of Endurance

Read 1 Peter 5:10-11. Ask: **How is God characterized by Peter?** (Peter refers to God as the "God of all grace," and the God who personally calls us to be His children. In other words, God is completely and absolutely faithful to His children. His intention is for our endurance of hardship to bring the fullness of grace into our lives. He has called us to participate in the glory of Jesus Christ, and He has done all that is necessary to ensure our place in that glory.)

Ask: **What will God do through our endurance of painful trials?** Explain that Peter gives four distinct actions God will accomplish for us through our endurance of suffering. Use the following information to assist you in your discussion.

Restore you = to make you fit and complete. Through our endurance, God equips us for life and for His service. He puts our lives together and supplies our need.

Make you strong = to fill you with ample strength. Out of His strength, God always gives us the strength we

need to face the demands of life.

Make you firm = to make solid, like a stone.

Make you steadfast = to lay the foundation, and sit us down on that foundation which cannot be shaken or moved.

Ask: **Thinking of your own difficult times, how are Peter's words significant for you personally?** Lead the group in a time of open sharing. Then lead the group into the "note of thanksgiving" activity. Allow group members the opportunity to express their gratitude for what God does in their times of enduring. Have them write their thoughts individually, then ask for volunteers to share.

GROWING BY DOING 10–15 minutes

Finding Your Footing

Have group members complete the activity individually. Then divide into discussion teams of three or four to share responses. Have teams spend the balance of their time praying for each other based on what has been shared.

Optional–Sharing a Touch of Hope

Ask: **What has impacted you most from this study of 1 Peter?** Have group members share one or more things. Ask for clarification or further comment as appropriate. After each person shares, have the group gather around and lay hands on this person, lifting him/her up in prayer relative to what was just shared. Conclude by joining hands in a prayer circle and giving sentence prayers of praise for the hope and courage that is ours through Jesus Christ.

GOING THE SECOND MILE 5 minutes

Encourage group members to continue to grow in the glorious hope they have in Jesus Christ. Challenge them to use this study as a springboard to make the hope and courage of Jesus a reason for joy during their own painful times.

GROWING AS A LEADER

All good things must end—even small groups. Unfortunately, many small groups begin with the false assumption that they will exist indefinitely. Many small groups wrongly assume that they do not need to talk about termination—it will just happen. Other bad assumptions are that if termination is never discussed, it will never happen, or that ending the group will be an easy process.

The fact is, every small group will reach a final maintenance level. It is the job of the leader to prepare the group for termination at that point. The better prepared the group is for termination, the more positive it will be. Here are some tips to consider.

- ❑ Build the idea of termination into the group's beginning by establishing the length of time the group will meet.
- ❑ By agreement, set up periodic evaluation points, during which the life of the group is reviewed and the group's covenant renewed or terminated.
- ❑ Agree together that at a certain point in time you will either birth a new group, or reconstitute the same group. Both are effective ways to terminate the function of one group, while continuing to provide for those desiring to continue.
- ❑ When the time comes, plan for a final meeting of celebration and praise. Ideas for this meeting can include:
  - (1) having group members share what the group has meant to them personally.
  - (2) inviting group members to give "gifts of service" to each other,
  - (3) planning a reunion dinner, and
  - (4) having group members share how each person in the group has touched their lives.